D0049611

THE THING ITSELF

RIVERHEAD BOOKS

a member of Penguin Group (USA) Inc.

New York

2008

THE THING ITSELF

On the Search for Authenticity

RICHARD TODD

RIVERHEAD BOOKS
Published by the Penguin Group
Penguin Group (USA) Inc., 375 Hudson Street, New York,
New York 10014, USA • Penguin Group (Canada), 90 Eglinton Avenue
East, Suite 700, Toronto, Ontario M4P 2Y3, Canada (a division of Pearson
Canada Inc.) • Penguin Books Ltd, 80 Strand, London WC2R 0RL,
England • Penguin Ireland, 25 St Stephen's Green, Dublin 2, Ireland
(a division of Penguin Books Ltd) • Penguin Group (Australia),
250 Camberwell Road, Camberwell, Victoria 3124, Australia (a division
of Pearson Australia Group Pty Ltd) • Penguin Books India Pvt Ltd,
11 Community Centre, Panchsheel Park, New Delhi–110 017, India •
Penguin Group (NZ), 67 Apollo Drive, Rosedale, North Shore 0632,
New Zealand (a division of Pearson New Zealand Ltd) •
Penguin Books (South Africa) (Pty) Ltd, 24 Sturdee Avenue,
Rosebank, Johannesburg 2196, South Africa

Penguin Books Ltd, Registered Offices:
80 Strand, London WC2R 0RL, England

"Not Ideas about the Thing but the Thing Itself," from *The Collected Poems of
Wallace Stevens* by Wallace Stevens and renewed 1982 by Holly Stevens. Used by
permission of Alfred A. Knopf, a division of Random House, Inc.

Portions of this book appeared previously, in somewhat different form,
in *The Atlantic Monthly* and in *Preservation* magazine.

Library of Congress Cataloging-in-Publication Data
Todd, Richard.
The thing itself : on the search for authenticity / Richard Todd.
p.   cm.
Includes bibliographical references.
ISBN 978-1-59448-851-1
1. Todd, Richard.   2. Todd, Richard—Philosophy.   3. Critics—United States—
Biography.   4. Authenticity (Philosophy).   I. Title.
PR55.T63A3   2008   2008025186
179'.9—dc22

Printed in the United States of America
1   3   5   7   9   10   8   6   4   2

Book design by Gretchen Achilles

In memory of my parents,
Samuel R. Todd and Miriam W. Todd

Contents

At the earliest ending of winter,
In March, a scrawny cry from outside
Seemed like a sound in his mind.

He knew that he heard it,
A bird's cry, at daylight or before,
In the early March wind.

The sun was rising at six,
No longer a battered panache above snow . . .
It would have been outside.

It was not from the vast ventriloquism
Of sleep's faded papier-mâché . . .
The sun was coming from outside.

That scrawny cry—it was
A chorister whose c preceded the choir.
It was part of the colossal sun,

Surrounded by its choral rings,
Still far away. It was like
A new knowledge of reality.

—WALLACE STEVENS,

"Not Ideas about the Thing but the Thing Itself"

THE THING ITSELF

Foreword

THIS BOOK BEGAN with a simple feeling, the sense that my life, and much of the life about me, was not "real." The quotation marks insist upon themselves because of course my life is real, and so is yours. The world around us is real too, all of it. They are building a Comfort Inn in the cornfield. The corn and the field are real, and so is the Comfort Inn. It is a real motel. The woman on the television who speaks with emphases that would make you think her mad if she were actually in the room ("Thirty-*five Iraqis* died . . .")—she is real, a real anchor. Her colleague ("What have you done with that sunshine, Chuck?") is a real meteorologist, or at least a weatherman. My automated reservations clerk, Julie, is a real thing of its or her kind. I do not have a Second Life, but if I did my avatar would be a real avatar.

Nonetheless things start to add up—an infinity of little oddities and disjunctions and . . . disappointments that conspire to make me think there is a scrim between me and the world, that something more substantial, more essential, lies behind or below or beyond the apparitions before us.

I may have a peculiar problem. I do suspect myself of a limited imagination. I didn't like cartoons as a child. Still have no appetite for fantasy. I prefer football to baseball, because of all our sports football seems most like life, the sluggers and the stars, the taking of territory. Novels that are about the age in which they were written are the ones that appeal to me, novels about people whose lives one believes in, preferably well supplied with furniture and food and social anxieties. "Damn everything but the circus," said E. E. Cummings. I hate circuses. Once, during a brief interlude of Mideast peace, I visited the ancient city of Baalbek, in the Bekaa Valley in eastern Lebanon. It is a spectacular place, with the ancient Roman Temple of Bacchus uncovered only decades ago, most of its columns intact, the engineering feat that erected them still a mystery. Here is what the site did for me: it made me believe for the first time that there really was a Roman Empire. So perhaps I simply have an overliteral mind.

And yet I think I am not alone in the apprehension that a distance yawns between us and a world we fully believe in, and, most alarmingly, between ourselves and something we imagine to be our *self.*

This book is not meant to be an inventory of unreality

(though inevitably some such accounting occurs); instead, it tries to think about the very feeling of unreality.

A book with a subject matter so broad paradoxically compels one to be brief. (If someone asked you to write what you know about the world you would think encyclopedically for a brief, dizzying moment, and then you would end up responding with something the length of a Buddhist koan.) Faced with the impossibility of inclusiveness, I have become no doubt wildly idiosyncratic. Nonetheless these observations do range over quite a variety of subjects. It has helped me (and I hope it may prove to have helped the reader) to herd them into four categories.

Part I: Objects, the literal stuff of the world
Part II: Places and what we seek in them
Part III: Society, the life we share (or fail to)
           as a culture
Part IV: That most vexed of subjects, the self

A word keeps trying to appear in this book. At first I shove it underwater with my oar, but eventually, unstoppably, it bobs to the surface. The word is "authenticity." I will not become ensnared here in an effort at definition but let it be heard itself as we go along. (It is tempting to paraphrase the Supreme Court justice on pornography: I may not know what it is, but I know it when I don't see it.)

The quality the term signifies is, I think, at least in our culture, in our time, a nearly universal longing. Authenticity is what we want from the world around us, from others, and crucially from ourselves. The quest for authenticity is the essential subject of these pages.

PART I

The Things of This World

1. The Lure of the Old

ONE DAY I BOUGHT A LITTLE BOX. What use the box had ever had was unclear to me, and really I had no use in mind for it. Because it was wooden and primitive and meant to hang on a wall, you would not have thought to put anything valuable in its four miniature drawers. They might have been suitable for matches or paper clips, or loose change, or whatever was cluttering up a tabletop nearby. I was attracted to the box only because of its proportions and its paint, a crusty salmon color that bespoke age.

I bought the box at the Brimfield antiques fair. Anyone interested in objects—in the nature of objects, if that's a concept that makes any sense—should go to this event, held in Brimfield, Massachusetts, three times each year. It is the largest such bazaar of its kind in America and quite possibly in the world. At Brimfield, people walk around with signs on their back saying "I buy ephemera" and "$$ for Old Toys," and dealers specialize in cast-iron stoves or ornamental lawn sculpture or oak furniture or advertising signs or manual typewriters or cookie jars. Once I saw a fellow who had driven all the way from Canada to sell items from two of his collections: wooden snowshoes and Coca-Cola coolers. You had to wonder how these interests had come together. You had to wonder about his marketing skills too, since he had so many snowshoes (hundreds of pairs, it seemed) that all by himself he had almost certainly driven down the market price, to the extent that there was, in the late spring heat, any market at all. At moments Brimfield looks like an amalgamation of every tag sale that has ever been held, or a cosmic version of one of those dreadful accidents you sometimes see in which a truck turns over and spills its contents along the highway. At such moments you reflect: There are so very many errant things in the world, and thank God for the prisons in which we keep them, for closets and attics and chests of drawers. For boxes.

But my box wasn't a container of anything, but an object in itself. A benign couple in late middle age, from New Hampshire, sold me the box, from their assortment of eighteenth- and early-nineteenth-century New England furniture. I paid a tidy sum for it: $200. Then I drove it home.

Sometimes things really seem alive. During the drive, only about an hour and a half, I felt emanations from the box, and they were not good. Something was making me uneasy, something made me glance over at the box and back to the road. I was eager to look at it more closely, and yet I wasn't so eager. Something was telling me the box wasn't what it claimed to be.

I detoured on the way home to stop by to see a friend of mine who is an antiques dealer. I showed him the box and asked him what he thought. He shared my skepticism and said he'd keep it overnight to have a closer look. In retrospect, I think he was being kind, that he knew at a glance what I was coming to realize: the box was a fake.

The next day he tactfully confirmed it in detail. The crusty paint? There's a chemical you daub on that will produce that effect. The nail holes in the back, stained with what appears to be rust—it's actually paint. The wood's been chemically "aged" too, as you can see if you look inside at the new wood behind the drawers. In fact my friend thought he could identify the maker of the box, a woman very much alive and specializing in such items. Months or even weeks ago my old box had been a little pile of wood in her workshop.

This was all kind of interesting, even funny, and we had a laugh at my expense. Of course there was also the $200, but I could discount that as a tuition payment for a lesson on antiques fraud. True, none of the lightheartedness dispelled that slight sense of a diminished self that occurs when we are deceived, for no matter how clever the con man, we always ultimately blame ourselves. And all the more reason to do so in this case, because, as I thought about it, no one had really lied to me. The sellers had said nothing about the age of the box, though you could argue that by placing it amidst their actual antiques they made an implicit claim. No, it was the box itself that lied.

If pressed, perhaps the gentle dealers would have called it a "reproduction." There is, after all, a distinction to be made between a fake and a reproduction: it is all a matter of intent. With the care that had been lavished on its nonaesthetic side, the "rusted" nail holes and so on, the box had clearly been made not to reproduce something but to pretend actually to be something. It was meant to deceive. As a 200-year-old object it would have been actually worth the $200 I paid; as a product of the twenty-first century it was worth—what? Twelve dollars and fifty cents?

One might ask why this should be so. The box I now knew to be fake was the same box whose look had appealed to me, and its color was still that attractive salmon, and in fact it looked quite handsome on my mantelpiece. That there is worth inherent in age is something I don't often question, but it's a proposition worth examining.

I was an easy mark, but suppose I had not been. Suppose the fakery was so brilliant that it would fool an expert. Oddly enough, I am not sure I would feel much better. In her skeptic's guide to American antique furniture, *Fake, Fraud, or Genuine?* Myrna Kaye describes one of the classic pieces of fakery in the antiques business, the "seventeenth-century" "great chair" actually crafted in the 1970s by a man named

Armand LaMontagne. LaMontagne, for obscure reasons, held a grudge against museum curators and he set out to embarrass them. He succeeded. He spent two months reproducing a chair modeled, with clever variations, on a genuine "pilgrim century" object in the museum at Plymouth, Massachusetts. This was not easy, involving, as it did, not only creating the chair but subjecting it to treatments that included burning, multiple coats of paint and paint removal, smoking, a brief attack with a knife, immersion in sea brine, and other time-consuming tasks. When he was satisfied, he sent the chair like a cork upon the waters downstream into the antiques market, starting with a dealer who was in cahoots with him. The chair changed hands a few times at prices under $1,000 until it was bought for $9,000 by the Henry Ford Museum, in Dearborn, Michigan. Then the craftsman disclosed his fraud. He was at first not believed, and was able to prove his story only when X-rays revealed marks that had been deliberately made with modern tools.

At this point one has to wonder: What's the difference? If the chair had the beauty of the original and the illusion of centuries of wear, is it not in itself a glorious object? Wasn't it just as good as the real thing? Well, no. We want something that is not "fake or fraud" but genuine. But why?

And why is one of my favorite books a volume called *Ford N Series Tractors*? This is an illustrated guide to the farm tractors made by the Ford Motor Company in the mid-twentieth century. I have such a tractor, an "8N" made in 1948. I wasn't actually sure it was made in 1948 until the book gave me the exact tools—serial numbers, subtle design improvements—to understand that all the details appropriate to the year were present on my machine. Thrilling. Not long ago I went for a walk and happened on a neighbor who was laboring over his ancient Dodge pickup truck. He was eager to share what he'd recently learned about the paint history of his truck. It had once been two-toned green, you see, and an expert had told him this identified it as a "spring special," manufactured only in the spring of 1953. He was thrilled too. Now Dodge trucks don't happen to interest me, so I could take only an abstract interest in his pleasure. It is disconcerting to realize that at any one moment all across the land similar obsessions bloom—about Barbie dolls and Walking Liberty half-dollars, about Bierstadts and old lunch boxes. Why? What does it matter if some more or less superannuated object is "all there," or in "mint condition"? Someone else would paint my tractor yellow and call it cute; I would take her vintage doll in its valuable original box to the tag sale and sell it for a dollar.

I know, or think I do, what the age of a thing means to me, but this quickly gets a little mystical. For one thing, if it's handmade it carries with it the presence of the maker, and the irregular marks of a 200-year-old plane, felt beneath one's own mortal fingertips, have the power to connect you with another time. Even old industrial objects, by virtue of having been held and used by other hands, have this effect on me. And then there are times and places that simply seem superior in the art of making stuff. For me, one of these is New England of the eighteenth and very early nineteenth centuries. A sense of proportion seems there and then to have been universal, so that everyday objects had a quality that today seems to require genius to achieve. "Around 1830, carpenters began to lose their eye," Lewis Mumford once wrote. Reading this sentence years ago I thought it remarkably audacious, but then I began to look around at the houses he was talking about, and I saw his point—pretentious colonnades attached to humble farm dwellings, windows a couple of inches too big for their façades—and what was true of houses was true of virtually everything else. What once was commonplace became rare and soon virtually extinct. (For a fascinating account of how this happened, see *The Old Way of Seeing*, by Jonathan Hale.)

I say all these things, spiritual and aesthetic, and I believe them. But they are not the whole truth. Others have felt just the way I do, and made the same points. And it is somewhat odd that in the history of feelings these sentiments have a rather recent provenance. A love of antiques only became a recognizable phenomenon in the late nineteenth century. It seems to have been a direct response to the appearance of manufactured household furnishings and the concomitant debate over standards of taste. Before that time one was more conscious of the condition of something than its age, and to go in search of an old piece of furniture would have been felt by most people to be quite bizarre. The story of how this happened in England is wonderfully told by Deborah Cohen in her book *Household Gods: The British and Their Possessions*. Despite the abrupt appearance of the collecting passion, it quickly took on an elaborate set of meanings that amounted to a moral fervor. Antiques required patience, discipline; they rebuked instant gratification; they stood as a barrier to social as well as manufactured fraud. "For the true cognoscenti," Cohen writes, "worshipping at the altar of fine antiques was no sin. There were false idols and then there were real ones." A collector named Robert Drane, a pharmacist by profession, did the world the favor of keeping a diary in which he revealed the depth of his commitment to the right thing and contempt for the wrong: Drane could denounce the spurious with the air of a fire-breathing preacher (his father had been such a man), calling a silver castor "ignorant, illshapen, cheap, mechanical and false in every respect." Antiques were, for Drane and his newly minted ilk, a way of repelling the falseness in all aspects of life. At the extremes of the obsession the objects took on literally a spiritual dimension; it was believed that if you listened hard enough they would speak to you of their earlier lives.

This is a lot to ask of a Chippendale table, but I am not unsympathetic. Old things sustain me in a way that I know to be not wholly rational. Around the room: a Windsor chair, a tall red case clock with wooden works, a brass bed-warmer. The chair's delicate splines are so fragile that I discourage visitors from sitting in it; the clock does not work, though I intend, as I have for years, to get it fixed; the bed-warmer has a tiny hole in it and couldn't safely hold coals, even if one were inclined to warm a bed. So, functionally, these things are marginal to useless. And yet I love them.

My deepest excursion into the things of the past happened with something that can't be called nonfunctional, though it started out that way: my house. A kind psychologist might have called the enterprise a "rescue fantasy," but there was more to it than that. When the place, a late-eighteenth-century Cape, came on the market, it had reached (almost literally) a tipping point: the sills collapsing onto the foundation stones, joists rotting in a damp cellar. The next owner was going to do something major (tear it down, tart it up): that seemed clear. I lived nearby at the time, and I feared the worst. Our cunning real estate agent may have pushed me over the edge with casual references to one prospective buyer who had grand plans for modernizing the old keeping room, with a Formica-topped island in front of the fireplace. I made an offer.

The upside of a neglected house is that often a lot of regrettable changes have not happened, and the real attraction of this place was indeed that so much remained original. The old symmetrical floor plan survived intact, along with much of the original plaster and moldings and, crucially, the massive stone chimney with three fireplaces, themselves made out of stone.

We (my wife and I) had only one rule as we entered this project. We would do all the necessary structural work but change nothing that was solid and had been there from the start. As to the necessities of modern life—stuff like a refrigerator and a shower—we would deal with those later, and we would relegate them to an ell. We didn't quite acknowledge it at the time, but we were attempting what they call a "period restoration."

And so we got under way. Of sills and joists (and the roof and the heating system, etc.) let us say as little as possible. Anyone who has done this sort of work knows that everything, once uncovered, was half again as bad as expected, and twice as expensive to fix. The more interesting problems lay ahead. As I say, the house was rich in original detail, but it nonetheless had undergone one facelift, decades ago, and then had endured some halfhearted efforts to reverse the changes. In a modest, countrified way the house had been Victorian-ized, probably sometime around 1880. The main change had been to the windows. They had been lowered from their proper place, tight up against the eaves, and the old twelve-over-twelve sash had given way to then newly fashionable large lights. They in turn had been removed (though one remained in a little-used pantry) and replaced with some cheap imitations of the older multi-paned windows.

By this time I had fallen under the spell of a true genius of restoration, a woman who was replacing some missing moldings, working with her collection of ancient hand tools. Like most geniuses, she was a person of definite views, and she let me know that the windows really should occupy their original space. She could make perfectly accurate new ones, and even fit them with old glass.

I resisted. In part because it was going to be expensive. And also because we seemed to be crossing a line from restoration to reproduction. But something had to be done about the current windows.

Then came a fateful encounter. One day I drove past a little house I'd long liked, and there was its new owner undertaking renovations. My God, he was tearing out the windows! Twelve-over-twelve, eighteenth-century sash. I stopped.

"You want to sell those things? 'Cause I'll buy 'em!" The negotiation that followed was, as can easily be imagined, comic, and for me hopeless. The deconstructionist who thought he was disposing of junk now thought he had treasure of inestimable worth: I quickly realized I'd been a fool, and tried to bargain my way out, with only limited success.

But I had my windows. And my friend and adviser, the craftswoman, was more than willing to strip and repair the old sash, removing and then refitting the wonderful old rippled glass. Surely this was closer to recycling than reproduction.

What better use for these sash than to keep them in town and in a contemporaneous building?

I'm glad I did it—the house looks as it looked to its builder and I have to think that is the way it should look. Still . . . there's an element of fraud in these windows, as there is, I came to understand, in the whole enterprise of period restoration. The problem of insistence on a pure vision is that so much life exists in the impurities.

There came a moment in what ought to have been the very nadir of the restoration when I felt a strange contentment. Nothing was done. We were months (years, as it turned out) from moving in. Some of the windows were replaced, but the old two-over-two could be seen in the pantry. We had taken down a false ceiling in the parlor to discover, as one always does, why it had been installed. It covered two layers of wallpaper—so intent had the Victorian-era owners been on creating a dark gentility that they had papered not only the walls but the ceiling with a lugubrious brown floral print.

My daughter was newly home from the Peace Corps and performing a mission of domestic mercy. She and I worked together. Steaming off wallpaper is always fun, and all the more so when it's overhead, with no place for the scraps to go but into your hair and eyes. We alternately laughed and cursed at the lunacy of it all. It was late winter outside, mist rising from the snow. How many forgotten souls over the course of 200 years had seen just this weather from this

room? The seasons eternal but each moment unique. For our part we had made the room uniquely a mess. But there was something about it I liked, with its plaster ragged around the windows and its wallpaper, emblem of someone else's keenly felt aesthetic, hanging from the ceiling. I felt that in a sense the house would never be better than it was at that moment, with so much of its history visible, and soon to be lost—lost, ironically, to restoration. I wanted to wrap the place in plastic and walk away.

Jean Baudrillard, the French philosopher, whose prose is one of those glorious Gallic unweeded gardens that ensnare you with their lushness, thinks he understands the problem posed by *les objets anciens*. He writes that people's affection for antiques derives from

> *the mythical evocation of birth which the antique object constitutes in its temporal closure—being born implying, after all, that one has had a father and a mother. Obviously, beating a path back to the origins means regression to the mother; the older the object, the closer it brings us to an earlier age. . . . Now, the search for the traces of creation, from the actual impression of the hand to the signature, is also a search for a line of descent and for paternal transcendence. Authenticity always stems from the Father: the Father is the source of value here. And it is this sublime link that antiques evoke in the imagination, along with the return journey to the mother's breast.*

If I ran an antiques business, which at my present clip I may be forced to do, I would keep this quotation prominently displayed as a kind of surgeon general's warning. The object you are about to buy may only exacerbate your identity problems.

2. Status

THERE IS A SIMPLER EXPLANATION for our love of the old—simpler, that is, than wombward longings. Surely to some extent I at least have these things because of the effect that I imagine they have on others. These relics say something about me that I want said. They advertise what I imagine to be my "taste." They may even seem to provide for me—perhaps this is in part what Baudrillard meant—a sort of provenance. One day a guest in my house, quite a distinguished person, emerged for breakfast. He had arrived the night before in coat and tie, but today, a weekend morning, he appeared in a Ralph Lauren sweatshirt, with the word POLO in huge letters across the front. He was, in effect, a billboard.

I want to be clear: this man is rather formidable—in his achievements, in his seriousness of purpose, and so forth—but seeing him in his sweatshirt I feel ever so slightly disdainful of him. Who would wear a god-awful thing like this?

There are shifts in cultural history unmarked in history

books. When did people begin to wear clothing with writing on it? Was this not significant? I visit a beach resort. There is a fellow sitting on the sand and his T-shirt says in bold letters: "Tommy." Is he Tommy? Of course not. Tommy is Tommy Hilfiger, the designer who writes his name all over everything and people buy it. Kate Spade puts her name on a purse and it sells for several hundred dollars. Calvin Klein enhances your underwear with his name.

One must not get haughty about Ralph Lauren and his friends. But it is tempting, isn't it? Where did they get their strange power? What did they do to derange people so that they actually pay for the right to wear an advertisement for what they have just bought? I do not wear clothing with writing on it. Even logos make me jumpy. The Nike swoosh, Mr. Lauren's polo player, Brooks Brothers' subtly intertwined double B's on a blazer button—they bother me. These things are meant to make me feel good, but they don't work. I feel in some crazy way virtuous about this too, though it may be the Old Fool factor at work. I remember so well a time when this just *wasn't done.* I went to school at a place where it was considered stylish—not, God knows, that anyone ever talked about it—to wear your "letter sweater" inside out and to cut the little red tag off your Levi's. As I say, the rules change.

And as I condescend to my distinguished friend I begin to wonder if my brand-phobia is itself an affectation. That is, surely I think more about not having these things than the people who actually buy them think about having them. And do I perhaps miss the point altogether? Is the guy who wears Tommy on his back participating in a clever, knowing, postmodern joke, whose unspoken text is that we all secretly care about labels, so why not acknowledge that in big campy letters? It may be. But I don't think so. In any case, it is not superior character that inhibits me from suiting up in Polo togs, I know that much, because I, too, have bought things for their social message. (Maybe in some way we buy everything in part for a meaning that lies outside utility.) And, no doubt like my brand-conscious friends, I have generally told myself that I was buying them for other reasons, because they were "the best."

When I was a very young man, I bought myself a leather briefcase. I have it now, though I seldom use it. It's right there on the other side of the office, beneath a table. Not just a briefcase but an English leather briefcase whose lid overlaps the sides. It's a true "attaché case" as they used to say, and suggestive of John Foster Dulles's State Department or the British MI5. But when I bought it I was neither a diplomat nor a spy; I was a very junior editor at a magazine. The briefcase cost an appalling percentage of my annual salary. It earned me some ridicule from those closest to me. Then one day, I left it open on a table at home and the cat used it for a litter box. This gave no little delight to those who had thought the briefcase pretentious in the first place. Luckily the briefcase was thick with manuscripts, all far less valuable to me than the stylish case in which I carried them (though I suppose their authors would have seen things differently), and it escaped serious harm. There were in the end some awkward letters to write. It is always a good deed to be a figure of fun, but the episode further eroded the pleasure I took from this extravagant purchase.

Yet, you know, I still think my now dusty briefcase is the very archetype of its class of thing. And perhaps, since the price for such an item has gone up impossibly, I can think of it as an investment, though in truth it was an investment only in status. When I see it at all, when it emerges from the shadows of familiarity, I look at it with a fond melancholy, a sadness for the young fellow who thought he needed this emblem to sustain his identity in the world.

That we use objects for display has been a truth understood throughout history, but from time to time the code needs explication. Thorstein Veblen's *The Theory of the Leisure Class* gave us the now venerable but still useful term "conspicuous consumption," of which my briefcase was an example, though not quite in the way he had in mind. In Veblen's view the things that conferred the most prestige on their owner were those that signified freedom from the need to work. Thus to have a lawn instead of a field demonstrated that you were a gentleman and not a farmer. The term "status symbol" was coined in the 1950s by Vance

Packard, the popular sociologist who made his mark with *The Hidden Persuaders*, on the wiles of the advertising business. Some of Packard's favorite instances of totemized consumer items were tail-finned cars, cobbler's-bench coffee tables, and mink stoles, whose charm now is retro at best. But the quest for the enhancing object goes on, even as the rules shift.

The landscape has changed in various and sometimes contradictory ways. It is now preposterous, for example, to own an expensive handmade watch. Toward the end of the last century it became possible to buy a quartz watch for about thirty-nine dollars that would keep better time than a handcrafted watch ever could. Yet people continued to spend thousands of dollars for what was essentially jewelry hiding a fatally flawed timepiece. In 2007, the *New York Times* managed to put together an entire glossy advertising supplement devoted to The Watch. It offered this rationale for the mechanical device: "A movement is like a living thing—a tiny machine with parts that spin and turn, keeping time, your faithful companion that depends on your involvement to keep it running. A mechanical watch is a link to the past." An advertising campaign emphasized that buying a watch was an act beyond acquisition; it was more nearly a curatorial act, as the caption to the soft-focus photo of a handsomely groomed father and son explained: "You never actually own a Patek Philippe. You merely take care of it for the *next* generation."

A recent updating of the game of status as it is played out among the near-upper class comes from David Brooks, describing the ethic of the people he calls "Bobos," for bourgeois bohemians. In his view the new class has subverted the old Veblenian rules. No longer do people want to show off their gift for frivolity, they want to show off their seriousness. They don't have possessions, they have gear. Brooks has formulated a basic law for contemporary upper-middle-class taste: "Only vulgarians spend lavish amounts of money on luxuries. Cultivated people restrict their lavish spending to necessities." He goes on to point out that "a person who follows these precepts can dispose up to $4 or $5 million annually in a manner that demonstrates how little he or she cares about material things."

In the home, utilitarian areas offer opportunities for high-minded expense. A slate shower stall, for instance, qualifies as a responsible embrace of the natural. But it is the kitchen that provides the ultimate room for self-expression. Brooks has some sport with these monuments to serious cookery: "When you walk into a newly renovated upscale home owned by nice, caring people, you will likely find a kitchen so large it puts you in mind of an aircraft hangar with plumbing. . . . You think you see the far wall of some distant great room shimmering in the distance, but it could be a mirage reflected off the acres and acres of Corian countertop. . . . La Cornue makes an adequate stove with gas and electric simmer plates for about $23,500."

Brooks is unsparing of his poor Bobos (of whom he admits to being one) and funny. But after a while, after the blizzard of brand names and the merciless hyperbole, I find myself developing an odd upwelling of sympathy for these hapless consumers, compelled, like most of us, to find what T. S. Eliot called in another context an objective correlative for their longings.

It would be naïve to think that the new consumption is any less ostentatious than the old, even though it has moved indoors—in a sense, become more private. In this, those in the upper middle class imitate the very rich, whose mores have also changed since Veblen's day. In a sense, the very rich have failed us by putting on a less public show of opulence. They no longer choose to impress the world at large with their wealth, thus depriving us of spectacle. They hide their luxury homes away. They fly on private jets from private airports to private places. Indeed one emblem of class distinction shone forth unambiguously. If a single thing could be said to mark the entry point for membership in the elite, it was the private plane. Not, to be sure, the lowly self-piloted sport plane, but the jet. Ideally, the Gulfsteam IV, with international reach. The very rich tend to save their displays for their friends. They may be wise.

Not long ago I was party to a bizarre scene as a guest at a house on a sheltered cove on the Maine coast. A yacht of some 140 feet lay at anchor. On its stern sat a helicopter. From time to time the helicopter would rise thwopping away at the quiet of the cove. A few minutes later it would return. This went on for a few days. The yacht was not native to these waters, and resentment stirred among the residents, none of them poor. It was the "nesting osprey" they said they were worried about, and I'm sure they were. But the intruder was annoying on other grounds too: this machine altered the social ecology. The flying yachtsman had reminded the merely rich of how very rich it is possible to be.

If we understand display only as a means to assert status, we miss some subtleties. Much of the time, all of us, rich and poor, choose our objects to make a claim not about our means but about our taste. Taste, even more than money, is the triumphant social weapon, and though it is hard to begrudge anyone his Viking range, there is a nasty side to this. The French social critic Pierre Bourdieu says that "tastes (i.e. manifested preferences) are the practical affirmation of an inevitable difference. It is no accident that, when they have to be justified, they are asserted purely negatively, by the refusal of other tastes. In matters of taste, more than anywhere else, all determination is negation." That is, my Kenmore range bespeaks a kind of lowbrow-ness that you emphatically reject with your Viking.

But Bourdieu may take too dark a view. People in their gleaming kitchens remind of us of something else, something that has no doubt always been true about ostentation. We often put on a show for an audience of one. Some important part of consumption is really about and for one-self. It represents our desire to enlarge, to complete, to reify ourselves. With our purchases, we try to become more acceptable not fundamentally to others but to ourselves. Ship-wrecked and alone, we would find water and food and, next, shelter, and then when we were safe in our lean-to, we would decorate it.

Things put us in a difficult spot. They demand an attitude from us. And yet when we seem to care about them at all we are said to be shallow materialists. A wealth of literature, and a powerful strain of American thought, condemns the substitution of objects for spiritual qualities—for love, for harmony with the world, for a sense of inner peace. And not just American thought, of course. Antimaterialism seems to be almost universal among cultures, even among those for which materialism wouldn't seem to be much of a problem. The natives of the Pacific Northwest have their potlatches. The ascetic Muria Gonds of central India engage in what one anthropologist calls "conspicuous parsimony." Nineteenth-century Europe, as it industrialized and developed a middle class, spawned a rebellion of the spirit that associated the accretion of wealth with the loss of the soul. Before he developed his systematic and comprehensive criticism of capitalism, the young Karl Marx wrote in his "Economic and Philosophical Manuscripts" with a passionate froth of mordant irony and dewy idealism, suggesting that money itself is a form of death-in-life:

The less you are the more you have. . . . The less you are the
less you express your life, the more you have the greater is
your alienated life—the greater is the saving of your alien-
ated being. Everything which the economist takes from you
in the way of life and humanity, he restores to you in the
form of money and wealth. And everything which you
are unable to do, your money can do for you; it can eat,
drink, go to the ball and the theatre. It can acquire art,
learning, historical treasures, political power, and it can
travel. It can appropriate all these things for you . . . but al-
though it can do all this, it only desires to create itself, and
to buy itself.

Thoreau spoke less drastically, in a way more congenial to
the American temperament. "A man is rich in proportion to
the number of things which he can afford to let alone," said
the saint of antimaterialism. Of course, Thoreau was always
more complicated than the apothegms we mine him for.
Think of the loving description of the materials he assembled
to build his cabin, their cost detailed to the last half-cent, and
of the pleasure he took in his three chairs. At another moment
he wrote, "Money comes between a man and his objects,"
suggesting that, removed from the world of commerce,
things have some sort of undefined but essential worth. Oddly
enough, one way to read this sentence is as a pithy and elegant
prefiguring of Marx's notion of "commodity fetishism"—

the idea that capitalism even as it created things sucked the life and meaning from them. Things became understood for their transactional value alone, not as products of labor or means to a useful end.

There has seldom been an era in America when someone hasn't argued the case that the simple life is the good life, as two of its practitioners, Helen and Scott Nearing, called it. Today the movement is called "voluntary simplicity." A book in this genre, *Your Money or Your Life*, by Joe Dominguez and Vicki Robin, asks you to think of the time side of the time/money equation. "Money is something we choose to trade our life energy for," the authors point out, and they urge you to calculate your expenses in terms of hours, not dollars spent. One can warm to such advice. But all people who pursue this course thoughtfully soon encounter a paradox: having fewer things does not lessen your preoccupation with things; it may only quicken in you an interest in finding just the right stuff. Indeed at the extremes of simplicity we may find ourselves becoming crazed about things, like a prisoner in solitary confinement constructing a fly cage out of matchsticks.

In the fifties, materialism seemed to explain just about everything that could go wrong with our world. Materialism was directly implicated in a loss of faith. It wasn't just their territorial ambitions that made the Soviets into villains: it was "Godless materialism," an ironic indictment of a society that was standing in line to buy potatoes. Such critics as Vance Packard (whose concerns ran deeper than "status seeking") and John Kenneth Galbraith chastised us for our addiction to manufactured goods. (The history of this sustained critique is told in Daniel Horowitz's *The Anxieties of Affluence*.) Packard pointed out that we had begun to look "a bit fatuous in the eyes of the world." In *The Affluent Society* Galbraith saw an almost addictive relationship between the rising middle class and its material objects. In the arch style for which he became famous, he wrote that our "wants are increasingly created by the process by which they are satisfied." There was a widespread sense—widespread among intellectuals and pundits—then that the largest problem we faced as a culture was its material well-being. (Of course, this was also the age when it was believed that Americans would die of ennui because the limitless automation of industry would continue to shorten the workweek to nothing much at all.) The indulgences of the middle class of that era look rather meek to our retrospective eyes. And only later, with the work of such critics as Michael Harrington, did the nation open its eyes to the existence of widespread poverty in its midst. In any case, all right-thinking people stood still and bowed their heads in chagrin for such tongue-lashings. Covertly, perhaps, they felt a little flush of pride to be worthy of such contempt, active participants in a culture so favored by fortune, so enviably flawed. In any case, they continued to buy.

We have achieved a marvelous doubleness of understanding, a perfect cognitive dissonance, on this subject. We
nurture our spiritual self-regard by deploring consumption,
even as we accept what is universally acknowledged: that
consumption is the engine of our well-being. No less a
leader than F.D.R. was the first president to urge us to restore
a lagging economy to health by buying stuff. He was not the
last. When recession loomed in 2008 the goverment mobi-
lized to assemble a "stimulus package" of tax rebates and direct handouts to get people to spend more. Never mind that
the targets of this largesse had already been stimulated to
within an inch of their lives by the very society they live in.
They had huge credit-card debt hanging over their heads
and mortgages they could not pay. The recession, after all,
was brought on by the irresponsible ("predatory" was the
term of art) lending practices of shoddy institutions, whose
paper was then bought up by supposedly reputable firms.

No matter. The answer was not to change our national
priorities, the answer was to shop. It helped that over time
things had grown strangely cheap. Through the gospel of
free trade gradually we found a way to enjoy our things
without the tedium and expense of actually making them. To
me the history of our dependence on foreign goods is a
story told in pockets. One day I needed (that word of infinite
elasticity in a consumer society) a new computer carrying
case, needed it in a hurry, on my way to the airport. Whatever else we have, we have a society designed to answer this

sort of problem. I stopped at my nearest office-supply store, bought the thing for something like $29.95. On the airplane I studied it. It had no fewer than sixteen separate pockets of one kind or another, exterior, interior, pockets within pockets, little receptacles for pens and pencils, calculators, and so on. I reflected that if you were to pay someone in the First World (the buying country) to replicate this feat of pocket-sewing, it would cost hundreds of dollars. But it was made in the Third World, by the selling country. The darkened airline cabin at 35,000 feet stirs long and not necessarily coherent thoughts. To think at all of the way products like my computer case (my computer, for that matter) are made is to think of human suffering. On the other hand, in an infinity of little sums, not enough to help the seamstress, we send our money away to these foreign places. Sooner or later perhaps we will pay a price for this arrangement, but not yet, not yet.

And along with irresistible discounts came the beguilement of infinite choice. My supermarket offers me a dozen kinds of Cheerios, uncountable flavors of dog food, and frozen pizzas various enough that you could eat a different kind every day for a month and half. My orange juice brand is well established in my mind; now all I have to do is decide whether I want it with no pulp, low pulp, some pulp, or lots of pulp, "light," or with calcium, or antioxidants, or "low acid."

Wouldn't it be easier all around to revert to the days when there were one or two kinds of everything? It would be—but the people in charge seem to know something. The modern marketing strategy of "consumer choice" is, I suppose, rather like the way in which a clever parent governs a child: Do you want pasta or rice with your broccoli? (Either way, you're having broccoli.) But it can permanently confuse us. The marketers are just trying to sell things, not (I trust) trying to distort our brains, but that may be the effect. It takes superhuman effort to resist this onslaught of stimuli—or more exactly this continual summons to identify and refine your sense of self through the consumer choices you make. They have a niche for people like me: they simply call one version "original," and, as they know I will, I buy it. Thomas Frank, who writes on cultural politics, puts the situation exactly: "Consumerism is no longer about 'conformity' but about 'difference.' . . . This imperative of endless difference is today the genius at the heart of American capitalism."

In roll the catalogues, filling the mailbox, and so nicely targeted these days. Ingenious Devices Inc, it's true, has me somewhat misunderstood—I am not much tempted by "video eyewear" that would connect to my iPod, if I had one of those, to give me a "virtual 62-inch" movie screen sitting right on top of my nose. But my menswear specialists at the House of Anglophilia know where I live, all right, and though I'm not sure I need the Lovat tweed shooting jacket with two-bellows pockets (with scalloped top for easy entry to shells), it's really kind of nice, and so are the chamois-lined rubber boots . . .

On the surface, we are a nation of anti-Thoreauvians. We flock to our malls, surround ourselves with gadgetry, gewgaws, and junk, worship our cars, our computers, our cellphones, our HD flatscreens. We revel in stuff, and when it bores us we replace it with more stuff. We forget to put the Christ in Christmas. We are terrible, terrible people. "Americans love junk," George Santayana is said to have said. "It is not the junk that bothers me. It's the love."

This diagnosis of our culture, so painfully familiar, I think misses the true poignance of our consumer habits. "No one ever went broke underestimating the taste of the American public"—true, true. And yet we are more complicated than we give ourselves credit for. For one thing, much of the quest for reality in everyday American life *is* a quest for the "right stuff," an effort to purge yourself of junk and fight through the ersatz to the true. It is like a continual test. We make it our responsibility to create a private beauty. One could add that we feel we have to, because public beauty continually falls victim to the sprawling commercial landscape. And unfortunately, the more each of us turns inward trying to outfit utopias of one, the more of a public mess we help to create, making our world into a Christmas morning living room, strewn with the wrappings of our toys. Each day the barges make their way to the sea, whose vast patience we test with millions of pounds of garbage.

One mistake that critics of consumerism make is to think that we actually want, or sometimes even that we think we want, the things we buy. Sometimes we spend to spend. Spending is agency and power. Not long ago I went shopping with a friend in New York. She wanted to show me a little store in SoHo, which specialized in a sort of urban rusticity much loved by young householders in Manhattan. It had stout-legged farmhouse tables, and reclaimed chests of drawers finished in milk-paint shades of reds and greens, and dozens of smaller items, a garden of tchotchkes. The things I liked best were the marble peaches, carved, the sign said, by an "Italian craftsman," a whole bowl of marble peaches and only $18 apiece. I nearly bought some, and had I done so it would have been for one reason only: to buy them. I had no interest in owning marble peaches at all. Later at another store, my friend did buy something: chocolate spoons. They were a dollar apiece—edible spoons that you could use to stir your coffee or perhaps eat a mousse. I don't know that she had a deep interest in the spoons, but they were fun to buy. It occurred to me later that more things should be edible. Suppose you could buy a new Mercedes . . . sorry, that's crazy. But the point is, there is a freedom in the kind of spending that leaves no trace, burdens us with nothing. Spending money without having to get anything lasting in return is part of the reason we have become obsessed with restaurants.

We are always assailing ourselves for being the most materialistic culture on earth. But like almost everything else we say about ourselves, it is a half-truth. In this country, founded on an idea, I think "we" have mixed feelings about our things—though we may buy them compulsively, something in us hates them too. That's the nasty secret behind the shoddiness of so much that we buy. We hate it. We want it to break and get dirty and wear out. We want to throw it away. And then, alas, we want to buy some more. We are like the uneasy smokers these days who, I notice, often throw their cigarettes to the ground after a few puffs. It is the lighting up that gives the pleasure. I sometimes wish we were more materialistic, not less. As it is, we like to buy more than we like to have. We take a nihilistic pleasure in obsolescence. Our country really needs to love the physical, tangible world more than it does, to care more about what it creates, buys, places on the earth.

People interviewed on television after a natural tragedy ravages their world—flood or fire or landslide—say, "It's only things, and things can be replaced. Thank God everyone is safe." And you admire them for this, as they expect you to, and their response is indeed right and good. But sometimes, hearing these ritualistic lines, I get an unworthy, even cold-hearted feeling. I want the things to be mourned. Many things, after all, survive us, and some deserve to, in part because they contain us.

Some other societies are perhaps a bit clearer on this idea. In the western Pacific, for instance, there is the concept of the *kula*, which refers to the way in which objects accumulate value entirely on the basis of who has owned them. The objects themselves tend to be collections of shells that have little or no intrinsic worth, until they are passed from tribal leader to tribal leader, when they take on the luster of provenance. Any serious thinker in the West wanting to give things their due has to feel the chill gaze of Karl Marx, reminding us that capitalism has robbed things of their soul forever. But some anthropologists lately have begun to take a fresh, curious, and one might say humane attitude toward things, and toward consumption. In his wonderfully titled anthology *The Social Life of Things*, Arjun Appadurai advances the idea that it makes sense to think of things as having "biographies," passing through various identities, so that they indeed take on a life of their own. An object's "exchange value" (the Marxist term) may thus over time be supplemented if not replaced by other meanings. "The commodity phase of the life history of an object does not exhaust its biography," he writes. This is not to say that most objects live outside the economy altogether: "Pricelessness is a luxury few objects can afford," Appadurai observes. I suppose that small category would include a piece of the true cross or a teddy bear so battered by use that its market would consist of a single child. But many objects, perhaps all objects, whatever their price tag, occupy a larger economy of feeling and significance.

I am inclined to agree with Leah Hager Cohen's view of things, as it unfolds in her book *Glass, Paper, Beans*. Cohen explores the provenance of the three things of the title, things that begin her day: the beans that make her coffee, the glass that holds the coffee, the newspaper she reads. Some 300 pages later we have visited a glassmaking factory in Ohio, a coffee plantation in the hills of southern Mexico, and the pulpwood forests of New Brunswick and met the people who produced the things. In Cohen's hands the border between the human and the material becomes more porous than we usually allow. She reminds us of the humanity invested in made objects.

Cohen has no problem with fetishism. We may deride the notion that things contain intrinsic meaning or power as the magical thinking of primitive people who would ward off evil with amulets and dolls. Cohen embraces the term. She says that "if fetish worship really is a behavior of savages, then we are every one of us a savage still, for we all engage in fetishism on some level." Cohen suggests that "the extent to which almost anything appeals may be the extent to which it signifies, to which it evokes and resonates with associations and meanings in our own minds. The more powerfully an object signifies, the more fetish-like it is."

This is dangerous territory, of course. Every couple of years it seems that somebody in Congress proposes that we amend the Constitution of the United States to make an assault on "the flag"—that is, on any individual American flag—a crime. As the debate unfolds, supporters invariably speak of the brave men and women who have "fought and died for this flag." Opponents gently point out that while no one approves of the "desecration" of the flag, we mustn't compromise people's right to free speech. No one dares say in public that the people who propose the amendment are insane, or so badly confused that they deserve counseling. The flag is not the nation. No object is an idea. The symbol is not the symbolized.

But there is a far more benign sort of fetishism, the significance that derives from the private associations things have for us, items like the shaving mug you inherited from your grandfather, your mother's cameo, the battered toy train that survived your childhood. There is a purity to such objects, and I want to see much of the world this way, and sometimes I do. Once it fell to me to clean out the abandoned and uninhabitable house of an elderly woman slipping into dementia. I threw away her broken kitchen stool. When she heard the news she reproached me fiercely: "We used to play choo-choo with it!" She was speaking of a childhood eighty years ago. I felt a sinking in the stomach, still do as I recall the moment. Anything, it seems, can be invested with humanity. But then one wonders, with a colder heart, what *about* the stuff that clogs our stores and homes, stuff that was (if you look at it in a dark mood) manufactured with indifference, sold with contempt, bought in delusion, to be thrown out in boredom and despair? What about the junk? And worse still, what about those things that by our own behavior we turn into junk?

3. The Tears of Things

AS VIRGIL KNEW LONG AGO, things contain the power not only to preserve warm memory but to evoke misery too. *Lacrimae rerum.* The tears of things. When we put false hopes in objects, then the objects, broken or abandoned, take us straight back to the longing, the foolishness, the self-deceit. Even derelict and useless, things live on silently accumulating meaning. Not long ago I contemplated leaving my house of many years. "Nobody over fifty should move," says the hero of Walter Kirn's novel *Up in the Air*, and he may be right. In any event it was necessary to clean out the barn.

Come out and visit this building. It is a Museum of False Enthusiasms. How many pairs of cross-country skis can a family reasonably own?—all of them now in disuse. The horse stall, never quite finished, though it all too briefly held a horse. Now that whole misadventure comes back, and I remember pounding the nails into the floorboards before the beast's arrival, tiring my arm until it wouldn't move. A revelation of weakness to my young self: a glimpse of mortality. And buying halters and curry brushes soon to be useless—there's one over in the corner. And here, look at this bright blue bucket, a feeding bucket with a flat back so it can hang straight against a wall. Just a piece of plastic but it was given to me by my youngest daughter. How the heart rises in love, but it is love mixed with guilt. I disappointed her. The bucket was for the sheep we raised, but after a couple of seasons we lost too many lambs and I lost the will to care for them. The bucket, given in innocence, sits here, an emblem of fecklessness.

And over here two wagon wheels, their spokes too rotten to preserve, taken from a relic I found in the woods at the edge of the field, where it had been drawn one last time and abandoned. How had its owner allowed it to fall into such disrepair? I know, all too well. Even the wheels stir rueful memories. I should have just left them on, to give someone else the pleasure I had in finding the ghostly wagon, slowly losing its integrity, making the imagination fill in the missing pieces.

From a post hangs a set of tractor chains. Hell to put them on. The last time I did was on a bitter, knuckle-skinning day in December and I was helped immeasurably by a young guy who was in love with a daughter of mine. I never let him know how much I appreciated it.

Hanging in the corner, a bizarre thing: a Swiss cowbell! Oh yes. Given to me by quite an attractive woman. What did she have in mind? We'll never know. I should throw it out, but how really do you throw out a cowbell? Up in the barn loft— sap buckets, milk cans, broken chairs, and spavined tables. One of the tables threatens to dump to the floor an assortment of manual typewriters I once assembled. Folly, folly. Here is an antique flour sifter—in God's name, what am I going to do with this? And over in the corner I see the saddest thing, and not even mine. The huge yellow wings of a model airplane. It was built by the boy who helped me with the tractor chains. The boy is dead, as it happens, killed in a traffic accident. He was a better fellow than I gave him credit for and in some unspoken but real way I was cruel to him. Lord, get me out of here. I would like to be—where? In some place of perfect impersonality, in a business-class lounge at Heathrow, in a Sheraton Hotel room in Malaysia—in one of those places where you feel pleasantly deracinated, and where you think with warm simplicity of . . . home. Yet just now home is a place full of things that only remind me of my own insubstantiality. And for this moment these wretched, useless objects seem to be the realest things in my life.

4. Objets d'Art

IT HAS BEEN SOME SEVENTY YEARS since Walter Benjamin published his now classic essay "The Work of Art in the Age of Mechanical Reproduction." Benjamin declared that photographs and films and mass reproduction of images through printing were robbing art of that mystical sense of privilege it had long enjoyed as the work of unique genius. "That which withers in the age of mechanical reproduction," he wrote, "is the aura of the work of art."

Benjamin says all sorts of wonderful things in the essay, about the nature of film and mass taste and fascism, but the central phenomenon he describes has simply not happened. Yes, we have been bombarded with images, indeed to an extent he couldn't have imagined—he was writing before television had begun to do its work—but somehow this only seems to have enhanced the mystique, the aura, of original art. In recent years prices for paintings increased as never before in history, and art became one of the great trophies, a way for the richest to set themselves apart. But its attraction was not measured in money alone. People of all sorts flocked to museums to see traveling shows of great paintings. And the rarer the paintings were—those from the limited trove of Vermeer or Caravaggio, for instance—the more popular the show.

Contemporary art for all its irreverence has not shaken belief in originality and genius. Nor has it really wanted to, despite its pretenses. Jasper Johns once said, "A painting should be looked at in the same way that we look at a radiator." (I cannot be the first unkind person to remark that this was easier to do with the early work of Jasper Johns than with most paintings.) With his conceptual collages and stenciled words, Johns did what he could to break down the barrier between the trite and the unique, and to make painting into transparent thought. Then along came his younger admirer Andy Warhol, who did it right.

Warhol said of his Campbell's soup cans, "I wanted to paint nothing. I was looking for something that was the essence of nothing and that was it." The first soup cans, a set of thirty-two small individual paintings, were sold to a California gallery owner, Irving Blum, for $1,000. He sold a half dozen of them, for $100 apiece, before he began to feel a sense of loss when he looked at the wall. He set about successfully buying them back from his clients, and maintained the set. (A smart move, of course—they ultimately sold for several hundred thousand dollars and are worth far more today.) Although the soup can paintings were the art world's favorite whipping boy, their power gradually became self-evident.

Warhol was never indifferent to money, though he had little use for people who judge a painting by its price. He once said, "I like money on the wall. Say you were going to buy a $200,000 painting. I think you should take that money, tie it up, and hang it on the wall. Then when someone visited you the first thing they would see is the money on the wall." Yet he sensed the worth of his own work from the start. He was furious when a friend, to whom he'd given one of his early Marilyn Monroe paintings, sold the work for a few hundred dollars. "You should have held on to it. You would have made a lot of money," he said, angrily and correctly.

One way to look at the career of Andy Warhol is as a long playful inversion of Benjamin's essay. Warhol took those objects and those faces made banal by reproduction (the soup cans, Monroe, Jacqueline Kennedy, Elizabeth Taylor, Coke bottles), and he reclaimed the images for art. He made constant jokes on repetition: "Paintings are too hard," he said. "The things I want to show are mechanical. Machines have less problems. I'd like to be a machine, wouldn't you?" The silk-screened images of Marilyn or Liz are all the same but all different, off-register in this way or that, differing thicknesses of paint applied and so forth. When you see them—see them in the flesh, not reproduced!—the paintings give great pleasure, the pleasure of something transformed by vision, seen afresh, by a particular human eye.

Meanwhile, the genius of mechanical reproduction rolls on. In the mail comes a letter from Harvey Kalef, chairman and founder of Atelier America Incorporated. The company produces paintings, called "Brushstrokes Originals," which are in fact not originals but reproductions, in oil, of well-known paintings such as Van Gogh's *The Starry Night*, or Monet's *Regatta at Argenteuil*. They are created by some mechanical means that is described only as "a revolutionary replication process," and then enhanced by "our professionally trained artists."

It is hard to write about this kind of enterprise without sounding, as I now do, snooty. If you know anything, you know that you should disapprove of reproduction art.

You and I would not dream of having such a painting on our walls. We might, it's true, hang a print of a famous painting, but almost certainly it would be a poster that clearly identifies itself as a poster, usually one commemorating a museum exhibition. The license for having that very lovely but very familiar Cézanne on the wall is that it comes from "Cézanne to Picasso/The Metropolitan Museum of Art, September 2006–January 2007." Such a wall hanging suggests a message one is happy to communicate. Not "I aspire to fool you into thinking I own a valuable piece of art." Or not even "I like good paintings." But instead "Though

unable to afford original works of great value, I am a cultivated person who goes to museums and has seen the real
thing." Reproductions, in a word, are vulgar; posters that include reproductions are stylish.

The Brushstrokes reproductions actually appear to be
quite good. Clearly they are better in quality—that is, more
like the original—than a simple print. They have more
depth and texture—they are, after all, oil on canvas—and if
you were from Mars, or perhaps even if you weren't, seeing
them for the first time, you would gain more aesthetic
pleasure. But once you knew their true identity, this response would be canceled out by another feeling—a kind of
social shame, the sense that your pleasure was in some way
fraudulent.

But now suppose these reproductions were very, very
good. Suppose they were so good that the best art historians
in the world seeing the original and the reproduction next to
each other could not tell them apart. Something like this situation has already occurred when works of art have been
successfully forged, with sometimes amusing, sometimes
unsettling results.

Rodin once sued an art dealer for selling an imitation of
one of his works, only to discover that the fake was real; he
had forgotten he made it. Not long ago the *New York Times
Magazine* explored the phenomenon of twentieth-century
art forgery, in an article that asserted that somewhere between 10 and 40 percent of the paintings sold as the work "by

significant artists" are in fact fake. The piece used the case of John Myatt, a painter unsuccessful with his own work who discovered he had a gift for doing quick, efficient, and convincing imitations of diverse modern artists including Giacometti, Matisse, and Braque. Myatt was the painter, but he was not the schemer; he was in fact the tool of a brilliant criminal named (or aliased) John Drewe, who had a genius of his own for document forgery, through which he gave the new paintings their provenance. The vital importance of provenancing in the art world demonstrates what everyone knows in his heart: that it is relatively easy to create fakes. Not that just anyone can do it, but it can be done, and sometimes brilliantly. A conspiracy of the blind eye helps to perpetuate this situation. Myatt's forgeries were said in fact to be rather mediocre. But some of the people who thought so were the dealers who nonetheless bought them, claiming to be convinced by the documentation.

Supposedly the greatest forger of the modern age was a man who took on a task that would seem to be more difficult than imitating cubism or expressionism. He was Han van Meegeren, who in the 1930s and 1940s painted heretofore undiscovered "Vermeers" so brilliantly that they fooled virtually everyone. At that point, of course, one has to wonder: If the painting is thus so beautiful, is it not a thing of value in its own right? Van Meegeren himself put this rather poignantly after a trial, in 1947, convicted him of forgery. "Yesterday this picture was worth millions of guilders, and

experts and art lovers would come from all over the world
and pay money to see it. Today, it is worth nothing, and nobody would cross the street to see it for free. But the picture
has not changed. What has?"

This conundrum brought great pleasure to a notable
American intellectual, the late Edward C. Banfield, a professor of government at Harvard. Banfield once undertook to
do a study of the National Endowment for the Arts, which
was meant to guide the institution's policy toward support of
museums and artists. The result became a book called *The
Democratic Muse,* which, to say the least, failed to please the
NEA. Banfield questioned one of the basic tenets of the Endowment's existence—the value of original art in a democratic society. He suggested that museums overrate the
authentic at the expense of the beautiful. "The cult of the
original," he argued, was of fairly recent origin and created
by forces external to art: by "investment and antiquarian interests and of the consequent growth of art history as a
scholarly discipline." If reproductions of great pieces of art
could be placed in museums all over the country, he said,
they would afford the mass audience a chance to see a variety of work it might otherwise never experience, and this
would be a fine (and cost-effective) contribution to cultural
life. "Yet imagine the howls from the art world," he wrote,
"if someone were to propose that state and federal govern-
ments, rather than subsidizing the purchase of original
works of art for museums and public buildings, support

efforts to improve the quality of reproductions, perhaps by research to find better technologies, and to make high-quality ones readily available. Why should public art museums not substitute perfect or near-perfect reproductions for originals, thus drastically reducing the ever-increasing costs of security and conservation?"

If Banfield was being mischievous, there is no indication that he was being satirical; there is in fact every indication that the scholar, known for his hyperrationality on other topics, was quite serious. *The Democratic Muse* was written more than twenty-five years ago. Today its suggestions are less theoretical. Thanks to computer imaging, the technology is at hand to reproduce physical shapes with astonishing accuracy. Car designers, for example, can transmit digitized shapes to a distant office, where a model can be created. Of course it is one thing to extrude plastic and another to carve marble. But suppose you really could, for instance, replicate Michelangelo's *David* not just accurately but exactly. Would it not make some sense then to go ahead and do it, and to substitute the reproduction for public display while locking up the original for safekeeping? (After all, the *Pietà* was defaced years ago by a madman wielding a hammer and it now sits grotesquely shielded by bulletproof plastic.) And then wouldn't the same be done to all the world's greatest sculpture? The technology for paintings is harder to imagine, but it is happening in a crude way, as the Brushstrokes people have demonstrated. Suppose these methods, too, reached

perfection. Might one not go on to make at least one copy of the best of paintings, just as a precaution? And then, wouldn't you again be inclined to use the copy to protect the original from danger? Thus the *Mona Lisa* might emerge from behind her bulletproof glass, to be hidden forever in a vault and visited only by scholars, and replaced with the perfect copy. Crowds would presumably still flock to its place at the Louvre, and then it would occur to someone else to ask: Why not ease the crowding by doing two or three reproductions? And once one did that, then every major museum in the world would reasonably want a perfect *Mona Lisa* of its own.

Mona Lisa, to be sure, is rather a special case, a painting so iconic as to represent all Painting, and as such somewhat disembodied already. It is in fact very hard to see, in part because it is forever surrounded by a crowd, because of its security protection, and perhaps most of all, because you can't help thinking: I am looking at the most famous painting in the world, at which point you start thinking of the parodic versions of it that you have seen, Mona Lisa with a mustache and so on. But think of a less celebrated painting, one that you love. Would something be lost if you knew you were looking not at it but at a perfect copy? I think so, but what?

One instance of reproducing a major work of art for viewing by the public already exists, but it constitutes a

special case, inasmuch as its creator (or creators) is anonymous and has in fact been dead for 15,000 years. When the caves at Lascaux, France, were discovered in the midtwentieth century, the Stone Age paintings in them soon became famous, and people understandably wanted to visit them. Lucky were those who did so, because now it is impossible, unless you are a "qualified" person. Public tours of the caves threatened to do what millennia of neglect had not achieved—the paintings were being destroyed by the humidity generated by all the visitors. So the site had to be closed. But the French government could scarcely pretend the caves were not there, and public curiosity had in some way to be satisfied. The French solved the problem by creating a perfect replica not far from the actual site. (This was not, it would seem, the only possible solution: they could have copied the paintings in a museum setting.) Now you descend into the earth to find dimly lit chambers with what appear to be rock walls and the elegant spare drawings of ancient beasts painted upon them. But it is all a reproduction. A center nearby explains how the caves were constructed—the micro-measurements that were done of the entire interior of the original so that the replica would be exact down to every last dimple and crevice in the rock. You might well ask what difference it makes if a random hole in a rock is in fact duplicated exactly, when the only thing of interest about the caves is the art. But then again, once you had decided to duplicate the caves, where would you stop, even though you knew that at some level or other the whole effort was crazy? I entered the artificial caves one summer day. I am not sure that I was improved by this experience. All I could think of was the effort that had gone into creating an elaborate stage set. I think I would have been content to know that paintings existed underground and that I simply did not qualify to see them. Like the North Pole or the Mariana Trench, it could be one of those places on earth that one is happy to comprehend in the abstract, to imagine, without ever visiting. It turns out that the visitors' center becomes the real highlight of your trip to Lascaux—or so you tell yourself, trying to understand what it is exactly that you have seen.

It seems to me that a similar sense of dislocation would afflict the visitor to one of Edward Banfield's democratic museums of reproduced art. Banfield may inadvertently suggest the reason himself, in one of the more amusing provocations of the book. At one moment he sallies forth at what he takes to be the intellectual snobbery and hypocrisy of the art world and its true believers. "Many people would never dream of having a 'fake' Rembrandt on their walls, however high its quality, yet own and enjoy record sets of the Beethoven symphonies." In eliding music and visual art Banfield only reminds us of the difference. The performance of a symphony—though it is the only way the music can be enjoyed—is not the symphony itself. In a sense every performance is inferior to the ideal form of the symphony, and the act of striving toward unattainable perfection accounts for some of the power of performance. But in visual art the performance and the creation are one. Much of what affects us in a painting or a statue is the knowledge that the performance happened just once, that it is of its time and only its time, and yet it is preserved for us. (Adam Gopnik, in *The New Yorker*, has written quite tellingly about this quality of art, that though we are taught that it is universal and timeless, we in fact cherish it because it is "a permanent experience of a particular moment.") How can we tell the dancer from the dance? Yeats posed a fine question—if you're thinking about the dancer. But if you're thinking about the dance, the answer is easy: the dance can be performed, better or worse, by someone else. But the painting is the painting is the painting.

Banfield fails to see what is unique about the visual arts. Michelangelo's *David,* Monet's Haystacks, Picasso's *Guernica*: in the beginning and in the end these are objects, transcendent objects but objects nevertheless. One way to think of such a work of art is that it represents the *ultimate* thing. Art is to objects as sainthood is to people. Most people can't be saints, and most objects can't be art, but in each case the extent to which they are marked by an impulse toward grace is a measure of their worth. Here those who would have us forsake the material world are on truly difficult ground, because in art we face the inescapability, the irreducibility, of the tangible, perishable world. Art sends us back to that world with a renewed eye and sharpened appetite. Art justifies our hunger for the real thing.

We need to be better materialists.

PART II

There, There

1. *Touring*

AFTER A LONG MORNING'S DRIVE through the Umbrian hill country, you have happened upon an inn. Is it open for lunch? You're in luck. Moreover, what a pleasant place it turns out to be—the rough stone walls, the crisp table linen and abundant glassware. The waiter seems to speak only Italian, at least he is grateful for your own efforts, and con versation in that seductive language is heard all across the room. This is very good, and the menu is appealing too in its simplicity, and as you sip your Montepulciano and dip your crostini in olive oil in anticipation of the tagliatelle funghi to come, you and your companion smile a complicit smile: you are really here, you have never felt so much a part of Italy before.

For what happens next there should be a precise word, be- cause it is a pain so acute, specific, and at bottom ridiculous. What happens is that another couple arrives and is seated (out of some misbegotten kindness?) next to you. They are speaking English. Really they are speaking American, and you could be more accurate than that: judging by their *o*'s and *s*'s you can tell that they come from the Midwest, probably from Minnesota. It occurs to you in a fleeting moment that although you don't like knowing this, you would be very pleased with yourself if you had such a fine knowledge of Italian regional accents. You feel churlish for letting these poor people bother you, and you realize that they are probably just as disappointed to see you as you are to see them. At that, you manage a weak smile in their direction, an acknowledgment of defeat. The smile is returned, and the moment ends in rueful comedy.

What is it exactly that we want from travel? Travel is felt to be self-improving, and I have certainly derived warmth from the notion, though that itself is a feeling about which one has to be cautious. Travel makes you more interesting to yourself, certainly, but not necessarily to others. (This is well understood by anyone who has made the mistake of saying, "Tell me about your trip" to a literal-minded friend.) Travel affords a kind of liberation. People speak of "escape" and at its best travel provides escape from more than the mundane or the tedious. Exhilarating moments abroad don't depend on spectacle or adventure—it is enough sometimes simply to feel wonderfully unimplicated in the world. I don't mean in the callous sense of being indifferent to suffering or injustice.

I mean only that one's identity floats free of its surroundings. At home, the embarrassments and shortcomings of your own neighborhood (or town, or nation) are your failures too; abroad one can gaze upon so much more that is only, but sufficiently, interesting.

But travel is not without its discontents, of which the anxiety in the Italian restaurant is a symptom. When it began publication, in 1987, *Condé Nast Traveler* declared that it was to be a magazine meant "not for the tourist but the traveler." Good idea, since that, it seems, includes everyone in the world, at least if we are to be judged by our desires. To be a tourist is to be docile, superficial, one of a herd. No one wants to be a tourist. "Tourists are vulgar, vulgar, vulgar," said Henry James, who traveled, or thought he did.

The distinction often seems precarious. Both traveler and tourist are, by definition, separate from their environment. We like to think that the role we aspire to, the traveler, has that distance on the scene that implies vision and understanding, while the tourist suffers the alienation of the passive viewer, the "sightseer." At its worst, tourism is felt to represent a moral or spiritual failing. And in our heart we fear that we, too, are tourists.

Some of the animus of Daniel Boorstin's much-praised book *The Image,* published in 1962, is devoted to contempt for modern travel, and for those who succumb to its bland charms. Boorstin laments the "insulation" that all the mechanisms of travel—airlines, hotels, tour "packages"—provide for the traveler, arguing that for most people travel is a matter of clinging as tightly as possible to the comforts of home in a foreign place. When Boorstin was writing, the Hilton hotel chain was in its ascendancy and a favorite villain of critics of popular culture. In a typical passage, Boorstin writes, "Out-of-doors the real Turkey surrounds the Istanbul Hilton. But inside it is only an imitation of the Turkish style. The hotel achieves the subtle effect, right in the heart of Turkey, of making the experience of Turkey quite secondhand."

In truth, Boorstin's indictment now seems rather conventional. The contempt that Boorstin felt for the herd of tourists has been internalized by the herd itself. Everyone, it seems, is looking for the "real" place, and for the real way to visit it. It's not as easy as stepping outside the Hilton. One reason this is so was foreseen by Boorstin himself—the proliferation of artificial experiences arranged for the benefit of tourists wherever they are around the globe. The beach luaus, the tribal rain dances, the horse-drawn sleigh rides, all those contrivances put on by an indigenous population to dramatize their lives for outsiders, usually in ways that represent not their actual life but a re-created, or imagined, past. The sophisticated tourist shuns such attractions by instinct, and still the problem does not go away.

Once I visited the little Spanish town of Ronda in the

hills of Andalusia. There were just two of us traveling (or touring), and though it was summertime it was an unusually quiet Sunday afternoon, no other visitors, and precious few residents, in sight. I hadn't just stumbled on this rather well-known town, of course; I'd been drawn there by a guidebook. It is an unusually beautiful place—perhaps the somewhat melancholy word "picturesque" applies— because of its dramatic hilltop setting and the huge river chasm that divides the town, and the ancient bullfighting ring in the town center. Hemingway had one of his honeymoons there and said something to the effect that if a honeymoon was going to work anywhere it was going to work in Ronda.

Although none of the usual bothers of tourism were present that sleepy afternoon—no crowds, no importuning from hucksters or guides—I was nevertheless acutely conscious of my role as a tourist. Asking myself why, I could only conclude that one could feel there the presence of tourists past. I found myself using the word "eyeworn" to describe the way the town's much-admired features seemed to me. It is a slightly crazy idea, perhaps, but it was as if the stones had literally been eroded by stares.

Some time later I came across a book called *Consuming Places*, by the British sociologist John Urry. Urry takes my notion rather more seriously than I did. He speaks of "the tourist gaze" as a social force that actually does change environments. First of all, it alters the world by the simple choice of what to linger on: what is in fact picturesque, what is mundane, what is romantic, what is pure and what is polluted. And Urry is right about the ultimate power of the "gaze," if you consider the scope of tourism and the way it shapes economies and individual lives and, in fact, places. The change is not all damage, of course—tourism harms the environment much less than strip-mining, and it has been a positive force for the preservation of some landscapes. But it can be in various ways destructive. It undermines independence, indentures populations, institutionalizes humiliation. It is a self-inflicted colonialism. One can overstate: just as the coal mine does more ecological damage than the five-star resort, the miner's life may not be superior to the headwaiter's. Still. Tourism has caused lots of people to lament the loss of the world, their world, as they know it. I was once "leaflet-ed" in Dublin by youths protesting the proliferation of B&Bs in their country—not exactly the slaughter of the innocents but a cause that inspired some passion. The Greek Orthodox Church (John Urry reports) created the following prayer: "Lord Jesus Christ, Son of God, have mercy on the cities, the islands and the villages of this Orthodox Fatherland, as well as the holy monasteries which are scourged by the worldly touristic wave."

Urry's book was published in 1995, when tourism was on a track to become the largest commercial enterprise in the world, a standing it seems now to have achieved. If you look at this in one way, it occurs to you that in many parts of the world whole populations depend for their existence on, in effect, being looked at. It is an unsettling, even an awful fact, and one that we desperately want to suppress whenever we are one of those doing the looking, a part of the "touristic wave." Because, for one thing, if at any moment much of the world's income is being produced by people watching other people, then inevitably a certain (appalling) number of people are going to be spending their money falsely—to look at other tourists. People now go to quite extraordinary lengths to avoid the malaise of tourism—for examples, "slum tours," which take one away from the resorts of Rio to its favelas. Or "voluntourism," which lets you spend your holiday painting someone's fence.

Given the vastness of the problem, it may be small-minded of me, but I find myself worrying less about the swaths of gazed-upon—the swaths of landscape and cityscape and the populations on view—than I do about the heart of the gazer. But the two problems are intertwined.

Much of the world that I have seen I have seen as a tourist of a peculiar sort, a paid tourist. That is, I have worked as a travel writer. I don't apologize for this, but many people think I should. It's true that the travel writer operates under certain conventions and restraints, which like a lot of conventions and restraints encourage hypocrisy. The essential cliché of travel writing is a sentence that goes more or less as follows: "Here, away from the madding crowd of tourists, lies the real [fill in the blank]." A writer of any so-phistication will, of course, not want to commit such a sentence to the page, and indeed will go to some lengths to avoid doing so. Let's say you are writing of the Irish country-side in autumn. You might suggest that it has many pleasures, but that readers interested in seeing the "real Ireland" should go there in August, when German tour buses clog the road, because the Irish have managed to make tourism into something so central to their economy. A little joke, which fools no one. The same old trick. To escape the language of the cliché is not necessarily to escape the trope. In a sense it is one of the unspoken but understood duties of the artful travel writer, no matter what else his agenda, to point the reader to the places that are not overvisited, not full of undesirables, places that remain, as we say in another cliché, "unspoiled."

And how does a place get spoiled? Well, it is spoiled by people very like us, which reminds us of a further paradox of travel. On the one hand travel is self-enhancing, on the other hand it is rather sneakily demoralizing. We use travel (in vain) to enhance our image: "Yes, sure, I've been to Fiji, but not for years. I hear it's gotten kind of touristy." But though we wear our travels, when they are over, like badges, while we are actually traveling we suffer constant little erosions of self-regard everywhere we go. Because, fond as we may be of the notion of ourselves as "travelers," shrewd as we may be in our choice of destination and lodging and wines, we are aware of ourselves as part of that declassed, identity-blurred worldwide mob.

And there is another, subtler problem. We seek out desirable places, but we may find that the more they please us the more we fail them. We may on the one hand condescend to them: "Isn't this charming. It's so primitive." But on the other hand we often attribute to the place we visit an identity superior to the one we bring to it. That is, if it seems particularly agreeable, we cede some of our own claim on reality to it. We impute to it organic-ness that we lack. "For moderns," writes the sociologist Dean MacCannell, "reality and authenticity are thought to be elsewhere . . . in other cultures, in purer, simpler lifestyles." The very search for a connection to the uncorrupted other place is thus an implicit declaration of our inferior nature.

MacCannell is the author of an undeservedly obscure little book called *The Tourist*, which explores the spiritual woes of this rather forlorn figure who we all at one time or another have been. In fact, in MacCannell's view, we are tourists far more often than we are aware. You can be a "tourist" in your own home, watching television: someone, that is, who sees the world essentially as a spectacle and feels disconnected from the culture he is observing. For MacCannell, tourism is little less than an emblem of the modern condition. We seek immediacy, but in the very search to find it we create distance. "Sightseeing," he writes, "is a kind of collective striving for a transcendence of the modern totality, a way of attempting to overcome the discontinuity of modernity, of incorporating its fragments into a unified experience. Of course, it is doomed to eventual failure; even as it tries to construct totalities, it celebrates differentiation."

Yes, but is differentiation such a bad thing? I suggested just a moment ago that one of the great pleasures of travel is exactly the sense of detachment from one's environment that MacCannell laments: that liberating "unimplication." Yet how perverse we can be. Far from enjoying that disengaged curiosity that can turn all disappointment into a worldly shrug, we often find ourselves asking more of distant places than we ask of home. This is true, at any rate, of those places that are stereotypically the most desirable for the traveler: the Lake District, Provence, Tuscany. And especially destinations where we hope to find a simpler, more earthy, even primitive life: the Greek islands, Samoa. We want them to accord with our idea of what they should be.

I recall reading the account of an adventurous travel writer who went in search of a story among the native inhabitants of the Amazon basin, hoping to produce a portrait of a culture untainted by civilization. He traveled to the headwaters of the river, only to encounter there the sight of a small boy wearing a Chicago Bulls T-shirt. He wrote about it, and knew that what he was reporting was intrinsically interesting, and yet his dismay was real. When we idealize a place into a particular meaning, contradictory meaning pollutes the atmosphere worse than smog.

But suppose things go very nicely, suppose our destination lives up to its billing? Great. Though it's true that the more perfection we find in a place, the less we belong in it—the more aware we are of ourselves as "other" and, to repeat, often enough an inferior other at that. *That* must be why at bottom we so loathe and fear our fellow tourists. If there's nobody else around . . . well, maybe then we can get away with something. It's like achieving invisibility or repealing the Uncertainty Principle. We will be the disembodied observer, if we can just go unnoticed—no, more important, unmirrored.

As it happens, although I began to write this page in familiar surroundings, I am amending it in something close to a Perfect Place. It's a rural corner of France. It is "undiscovered"—not known to people like me. We have the use of a private house, which is surrounded by vineyards. In the evening we drink the wine that is made next door. I have driven for twenty miles in every direction and the countryside is unchanging, the vines yield to sunflowers and back to vines but the landscape remains a unified agrarian dream. Small villages complement the fields, each with a restaurant or two where only French is spoken. And now I find myself fantasizing . . . it is not enough just to be here, I would like to belong here.

"If you lived here, you'd be home now"—it's an old advertising slogan—and that, as always, would be the problem.

2. The Country

.

DRIVE WITH ME up the main road leading into my town, my actual town, the one I live in. There's little traffic though the road is broad, and we move along at a good clip. In fact the road is too broad if you ask me, the product of a misguided engineering project a generation ago. I'd greatly prefer a road barely two lanes wide. Only the occasional house comes into view as we go by. The houses, old ones, are a pleasantly organic part of the scene, a couple of Capes on either side of the road, a nineteenth-century farmhouse . . . I live in what I am pleased to call the "country."

Where is the country? For New Yorkers, or residents of other great cities of the world, country seems to begin once you get thirty or forty miles from home, no matter what happens to be there. From their privileged perspective, the city stands in marked contrast to anything around it. For others, the question is more complicated. To a large extent the country depends on absences as well as presences. Cows, fields, narrow roads, woodlands—all that, yes, says "country." But also, a certain sort of thing has to be missing for a place to qualify. A fast-food outlet, for example, compromises the definition, no matter how far it may be from Times Square. By 2005 there were about 12,000 McDonald's restaurants in America. Quite a few—but if you gathered them all up into one place (not a bad idea), even allowing for parking you could fit them into, let's say, 6,000 acres, just a corner of most towns. Yet the symbolic power of just one of these little establishments can radiate for miles. Battles have been fought over the arrival of the golden arches. Martha's Vineyard defeated them altogether; other places, such as Freeport, Maine, have fought to a draw, allowing the building but limiting the arches to a mere sign. All of this strife over what? Just 1,800 square feet of building and a parking lot. And the yellow arches. Why does this institution have such force? It is magical thinking, no doubt, but if you are a rural sort and a McDonald's looms up over your town, the chances are that you, too, will sign a petition saying that it "threatens the character of the village."

In our imagination the country is a repository of purity, of tradition, of simplicity; it is the enemy of modernity. But of course modernity lurks everywhere, and in most instances it doesn't really bother us. The eighteenth-century houses hold computers—so, for that matter, do the dairy barns, and a very good thing: it helps them stay in business. We are making our tour in a late-model truck, a marvelous piece of engineering. Somehow those inconsistencies, if that's what they are, don't affect us the way the look of the landscape does. Now we come to a house I would just as soon not see at all, a "split-level ranch" (the very name suggesting that it belongs elsewhere, but of course such houses don't belong on ranches, either). It seems to have been scooped up with a giant spoon from a suburb somewhere and dropped down here.

Suburb! That is the dread word. If there is one thing you can get everyone in "the country" to agree about these days it's that they do not want to live in a suburb. Amusingly, and kind of charmingly, this was not always true around here. We have a stretch of road called "Suburban Drive," so named decades ago when some wistful eyes looked past the cows to a future that would be more worldly and grand. The name has now become a mild embarrassment—I have no doubt that it will soon be changed, and though I'll welcome the change, it will itself signify a loss: in its naïveté, "Suburban Drive" evokes a time when the place was more fully "in the country" than it now is. Many rural dwellers who value their surroundings spend a lot of time fretting over issues like these, trying to reassure themselves that the country is where in fact they live. We watch like hawks for an incursion of anything that might be called suburban.

Born in the country, I nevertheless had a mostly suburban childhood. It's true of a lot of people who are among the countryside's most passionate defenders. This may give us a depth of conviction—it can happen here!—but it also infects us with a certain uneasiness about our claim to belonging where we like to be.

A slide show of my childhood houses would seem to depict a family in economic decline. (It probably does depict a family in spiritual decline, but that's another story.) It begins with a white farmhouse on a hill; next, a modest but still substantial stucco bungalow in a small town; next, a rather shoddy one-story ranch. In fact these dwellings describe the opposite—social progress of a sort: the difference is the real estate cliché, location. The final house represented arrival in a first-class suburb: Darien, Connecticut, infamous then for its "exclusivity." It's been eclipsed in both notoriety and affluence these days, but it remains a highly sought-after place, especially for corporate executives. ("Executive" is a word so overused and so vague that one hardly hears it, but I recall a time when it was fresher, and when it had real force in my life. My father was a salesman, and I desperately wanted him to be an executive. So did he.)

Moving to a new town is one of the best and the worst things a parent can do for a child. Much of what I know about social class I owe to that move. Before it I had lived in a dreamworld of homogeneity on "the farm" and in an unpretentious suburb. But it did not take long to realize that the new landscape had a logical organization, and the organizing principle was money.

The little house on Hillside Avenue, on the far western edge of town, provided my family with a toehold on a life they seemed to want but couldn't afford. That he had "a place in Darien" I know gave my father some status and pleasure in New York restaurants, but it must have been a hollow pleasure, because the fact of the house was dispiriting, and he could never have invited any of his friends or customers to see it. "I never thought we'd live in a house like this," I can remember my mother saying. This was decades ago, but if I stop for a moment I will think of the name of the contractor, whom my parents would periodically curse for the house's lightweight doors and cheap moldings. The worst of it, I think, the thing that galled them, was that we now lived in a "development" of sorts—there were five houses built on the same L-shaped design, varied in color and trim and orientation but essentially identical.

I was not immune to these feelings. I was ashamed of the little house. It is absurd (or worse) to speak of pain over such a thing—most of the middle class in those days managed to be fairly blind to poverty in the nation (not to mention the world), but still, a sensate person had to know that you couldn't really complain about your secure, well-fed life in a tony suburb. You couldn't. Yet even if the pain derived from lack of character, it was pain in fact. It appalls me all the more to realize I am not over it yet. Not long ago I drove past the house wanting to see it and then at the last moment wanted to speed by—humiliated by it still!

Meanwhile I made friends, and the friends lived in huge "converted barns" or in houses with decks overlooking "the Sound" (Long Island Sound), or in solid 1920s "colonials"— all of these terms as new to me then as items on a French menu soon would be—set nicely back from the road, with circular driveways. A few lived in the lushest part of town, in certifiable mansions behind high masonry walls, on winding roads, amidst dense greenery. For the first time in my life, I tried to make sense out of what had previously seemed a given, as natural as the trees themselves: the man-made landscape.

A Sunday afternoon fifty years ago. Three boys standing before a window, gazing out. We are each about thirteen years old. It is a wet, windy day in early spring, raw outside but scarcely unpleasant. In fact it is one of the most beautiful things I have so far seen: gray storm-tossed waves on Long Island Sound fill the view. I had seen the Sound only as a distant glimpse of blue from my classroom window; here it was face-to-face.

Framed in my friend's window, the ocean seems to be his. The furniture in the room is different from the furniture I know, plump sofas covered in striped fabric, a tall clock, a barometer, something I will later know is called a "butler's table." There is a dwindling fire in the fireplace. I can recall music on the "hi-fi," so apt it sounds like a bad invention: "Stranger in Paradise." (Not such a coincidence, really: *Kismet* had just opened on Broadway.)

The two other boys are my new friends. They are talking about their fathers. Both, it turns out, are presidents of their companies. (CEOs, we would say today.) It seems my turn to say something but I am wounded and tongue-tied. My father has never been in the same building as the president of his company. I blurt out a remark that can still redden my ears if the memory sneaks up on me: "Well, if my father were president of his company, we wouldn't be living here." As if "here" were some forlorn outpost of the petit bourgeois. As if it weren't the most wonderful place I could imagine.

The density this place had! In time—indeed before long at all—I came to see it with a wider lens, to see that it was an island of luxury, to see it as a sort of stage setting, to see it finally as a something very unsatisfactory indeed. But for a long moment, for two or three years, it was the world itself, and though I got to live in it I was not of it. I sometimes remind myself of the window overlooking the Sound when I want to speak disparagingly of the suburbs.

It is easy to dismiss the suburbs now. It is easy, and everyone seems to do it. In suburbia lies the greatest threat of falsity in our surroundings. In the suburbs it seems we can't ever feel we are in a "real place." Too bad, because a cold eye might conclude that "suburbia" has become the condition toward which much of the landscape seems inevitably headed. The journalist Michael Pollan (himself once a boy of the "burbs," now a country-dweller) not long ago wrote a telling essay on the subject of suburbia. He described a drive home from Long Island, where he'd been researching the subject, to his house in northwestern Connecticut:

I wondered . . . if what we used to think of as the fakeness of the suburbs hasn't also left its mark on the broader culture. To grow up on a "boulevard" conjured in a field is to be at home with the facade and the themed environment, with the quick-change and the quotation marks, not to mention the willing suspension of disbelief. It may be that ironic detachment is a mental habit we children of the burbs have come by naturally. . . . The funny thing is, the closer to home I got, the more omnipresent the place I'd been began to feel. Suburbia, I realized, is no longer somewhere you go, or leave. Wherever we live now, it's where we live.

But we hang on to the distinctions. I hate to admit how much "the country" has meant to me. To live there is to be credentialed, certified, anointed. It's an advanced degree, a trust fund, and a family tree. It is identity—borrowed identity, to be sure—which can be a problem.

I am a hypervigilant defender of rurality. I wince at the

merest violation, not only the split-level house but some small symbol of suburbanization: a false split-rail fence, a lawn ornament. In a place where bears are commonplace, someone decides to put up a front-yard statue of . . . a bear. This sort of thing should be actionable in my view. (That some of these offenses are committed by people who have generations' more claim to the land than I have is an irony not lost on me, though it doesn't alter my feelings.) Not long ago we had a flap around here over a proposed quarry. Many thought it would mean too much traffic, too much noise. The quarry didn't bother me. It seemed of a piece with country life. What bothered me was the sign in front of the house of one of the opponents that read "The Thompson Home Est. 1987." This is I guess a clever little joke on those owners of antique houses who put a date ("1795") on their houses. But the wrinkle-nosed cuteness and that cozy, self-approving "home"—oh no, I am not amused. The country has been violated again.

Part of the trouble with the country is that for too many people it is a place to live, and for not enough a place to farm. The existential approach to living in the country is, thus, to become a farmer. I have tried it. In that first rural incarnation I fell immediately into the romantic notion that people of the land are better people, and I idolized my farming neighbors and apprenticed myself to them. I drove hay trucks on sweltering July afternoons and spread manure in the April rain.

I raised pigs, sheep, chickens, and steers. It was a glorious time of wholesome stench and sweat and I was terrible at it. It was a wonder that my young family did not contract a fatal disease from the unsanitary conditions that prevailed on my small "farm." I use quotations marks, but happy was the day when I could remove them and did, because though the place was just nine acres, it generated enough income to be counted in the state census. Proudly I filled in Schedule F, "Farm Income." Faulty grain storage led to an invasion of rats, a calf died from the draft of a broken window, raccoons killed chickens, and I fed carcasses to pigs, risking the spread of God knows what plague. The electric fences I strung were constantly shorting out in unmown grass, and each time they did, a pair of Black Angus, Mike and Tom I think it was that year, would show up at the back door. On more than one moonless night I went out to greet them there— they were visible only because, like black holes in space, they were darker than the night. They seemed to want to come in, and I had half a mind to invite them, by this time well aware that I was a better host indoors than out. Some people dream that they are unprepared for the final exam; I sometimes dream that I am entering the barn, where I have forgotten to go for months. Three or four sheep, unfed all that time, await me standing at eye level atop piles of dung, their cadaverous faces staring at me with reproach.

After an interlude in the city I returned to rural life, this time with more land and fewer chores. And in time, with no witnesses nearby, I dined out on my farming experience. "Yes, we used to raise some Angus. . . . Let me tell you about the time we got heavily into butternut squash."

All places are stories, stories we tell to ourselves. We have no choice, because all inhabited places, no matter how pure, are in fact polluted with meaning. No place is one-dimensional. We share our environment with too many disparate people who are telling their own stories.

Let's continue our tour of town. Little anomalies present themselves, here a log cabin, one of those prefabricated structures that recall the Lincoln Logs that were so much fun in childhood. Who are its owners? With their architecture they say of themselves: I am rugged and independent. I scarcely live in a town at all—I inhabit the wilderness. Next, there is a rather pleasing new house, designed in the stylized lines of an old saltbox. But around the bend is a structure of glass and unpainted wood that seems to want to overlook the ocean on an island in the Pacific Northwest. What a relief, then, to leave this polyglot landscape and come at last into one of the region's great vistas, a big farm in a long valley, its white barns bright symbols in *my* story: a story of a peaceful, slow-to-change bucolic landscape. It is not quite enough just to have the farm—one wants the farm to be the dominant reality. And so my vision assembles other components—fallow but open land, dormant but still-standing barns—to preserve an agrarian landscape in the imagination.

The rural dweller wants things to have a coherent context. But "decontextualization" is a characteristic gesture of the modern world. Most of the time we adjust. We even learn to love the freedom of cultural collision that makes up so much of our experience. We develop catholic, eclectic tastes. There is much to love in the world, and we can take pride in the variety of cultural artifacts we can mingle in domestic interiors, in dress, in cuisine, even in speech and manner. But eclecticism in the landscape is a different matter. It takes a strong (or a stunted) aesthetic constitution to revel in a disjunction of architectural styles, ancient saltbox cheek by jowl with Mediterranean villa and split-level ranch on a "country" road. The landscape is literally contested turf, a battlefield of competing dreams.

At moments this can be amusing. One of my favorite settings around here is the junkyard and the tree farm. The junkyard has spread itself like a pool around Fritz's garage, a garage in which something sometime must get fixed, though it seems that things mostly get moved outside and left. Across the road lies Tom's tree farm, the little Christmas trees set out with military precision in ranks and files. What we have is a factory of trees and a jungle of machinery. Each alone would be unremarkable, even distasteful, but together they are (to me, anyway) completely pleasing, a weird version of that contemporary aesthetic ideal, the "working landscape." It would be nice to be able to see all disjunction this way, all composed into a pastoral harmony by the viewer's eye. But it's not easy. Houses, houses are the problem. What is that half-timbered Tudor dwelling doing on this bucolic stretch? In one man's vision the neighborhood may be an up-and-coming Scarsdale, in another's a well-preserved Old Deerfield. The eye struggles constantly to organize, to filter out, to say this is the reality, that is an anomaly.

Establishing a geographical context poses far less a problem in a city than in the country. For one thing, to some extent anyway, jumble and contrast create a satisfying urban texture. Also, the denser the population, the smaller the neighborhood need be to seem coherent. In the country an unfortunate house a mile away can affect one's sense of the landscape and one's place in it, but in the city your block, or even your building, can define you nicely, and you can turn a blind eye to the decontextualizers around the corner (unless of course they are armed).

Rural landscape, by contrast, often breaks your heart. But when it works, it preserves something as valuable as open space, or clean air, or unpolluted streams. It provides a sense of wholeness, an organic environment that accords with our deepest sense of the order of the world. There is something else: its patterns stand apart from conventional social hierarchies. In fact a well-ordered countryside embodies a species of egalitarianism. One way you can distinguish between a rural and a suburban place—and, Michael Pollan notwithstanding, I think you still can—is to ask yourself how well-off the inhabitants of a given road or neighborhood are. In the suburbs you know, or think you do, with some specificity, because the created landscape is in fact organized almost completely around social class. As you go from streets named Linda or Darlene, with their two-bedroom ranches, to the streets named after trees or poets and lined with two-story Queen Annes or Victorians, and on to the hilly neighborhood of the narrow and winding roads whose names derive from Indian tribes or early settlers, where the pillared mansions hide behind walls or hedges, you know where you are, because this is not primarily a trip through geography but through social strata. In a country setting, it's different—not that social difference doesn't exist, and not that some houses aren't a great deal nicer than others, but there are little redemptive surprises: wealth and modest means, or even poverty, are more apt to rub elbows, and you have a harder time judging people's net worth by the size of their house. And this is not jarring but agreeable. Agreeable because the houses look more like dwellings and less like symbols. In the suburbs you have little choice but to assert your identity through your social rank; in the country you may express yourself with your garden or your woodpile (or the rusted machinery in your yard), and the code tends to disapprove of ostentation. Here a house, big or small, may distinguish itself by its age or its relationship to the land, or its intrinsic beauty. Only in the country can one cling to the dream of a classless landscape. It is something worth saving, it seems to me. But try to save it at your peril.

3. *Preservation*

NO TRACE OF THE ORIGINAL settlement at what was then known as Plymouth, Massachusetts, remains, but there is now, just south of the contemporary town, a newly built replica of what is imagined to be the original "Plimoth Plantation." The re-created village itself has an interesting history. It began in 1947 as the result of a grant from Henry Hornblower, an heir to the brokerage-house fortune of Hornblower and Weeks. The first incarnation of the new Plantation spoke to Americans' ancestral pride. It was a trim little community of humble but tidy shingled houses, connected with walks made of crushed clamshells, a sort of Levittown for Pilgrims. It was just the kind of place a New Englander would want to have come from.

The difficulty was—as common sense would have suggested, and scholarship soon proved—that the village had little to do with any reality that might have existed three centuries before. To its credit, the Plantation over the years has enlisted the best researchers it could find and has listened to their advice and constantly revised the surroundings. They have, needless to say, been revised downward. Now the village consists of a set of wattle-and-daub huts, with primitive fireplaces emitting smoke through holes in the roof. They look like generic dwellings still found in many impoverished places in the world—and for good reason. They are what human beings without sophisticated tools, or time, or the support of an industrial society, construct when they need shelter. Indeed, it is now commonplace for visiting Third World dignitaries to look around the site in puzzlement and say, for instance, "This looks just like Namibia."

Plimoth is an extreme example of its phenomenon, the full-scale town-as-museum. New England has several such places: Old Sturbridge Village and Historic Deerfield, Massachusetts; Strawbery Banke in Portsmouth, New Hampshire; Mystic Seaport in Connecticut—in various ways they all seek to preserve and / or re-create the past in real-life proportions. None of the others is quite made up out of whole cloth, as is the case with Plimoth, but they all depend on certain inventions: moving of buildings, artfully reproducing missing paneling, and so forth. I am happy these places exist, for the impulse they express and for the things you can learn there, even though I can get a little sad about them too. It's the docents, maybe, women of a certain age in mobcaps. . . .

The feeling I have about mobcaps may be akin to a sour

spirit one sometimes encounters around here. My part of the country seems to honor its past more than most, but the constituency for preservation is by no means unanimous, particularly when it spills outside the museum boundaries and threatens to affect the way we live. There are people, some of them townsmen of mine, for whom the very word "preservation" is a red flag. Asked about his success in saving much of a New England town from destruction by development, a local official said, "The first thing is, I never use the word 'preservation.' I talk about economic development instead."

Why is the term so fraught? Press the antipreservationists for a reason and they are apt to respond with a common phrase: "I don't want to turn this town into a museum." The implication is that somebody does want to turn it into a museum, that soon we will all be living in wattle-and-daub huts. An anthropologist would find plenty to analyze in this debate along the lines of class and caste. It tends, like a lot of local debate, to organize itself around so-called old people and so-called new people—natives of the town and people who have arrived in the last generation (or even the last two generations). It is also perceived as a dispute between rich and poor, in this case the rich being the newcomers. None of these images quite accords with reality, but they are convenient for many of the participants on both sides of the battle. (In fact the "old people" could often buy and sell the new people, but the new people spend their money more visibly—or, to the old people, risibly—on cheeses and lawn care.) The new people are given to clucking over the old people that "they don't appreciate what they have." The new people will fight against a new gas station sign that obscures the view of the old town hall, against a farmer who wants to turn his field into a gravel pit, against those who want to tear down an old building because it's unused. The old people say "a man ought to be able to do what he wants with his land." The antipreservationists are not so blind as to fail to realize that they suffer considerable contempt for their stance. But they take it anyway.

As for me—no ambiguity about where I stand on these issues. Save everything! But I no longer experience my own inclinations with the same righteous conviction I used to enjoy, and I have come to think that the antis are not simply the obstructionists they sometimes seem to be. Dean Mac-Cannell has some pointed things to say on the subject of preservation. He argues that it is a characteristic gesture of modernism. In the act of trying to save the old from destruction, we are asserting our lack of connection to that world. The antipreservationists in town don't use that language exactly, but they may in fact be feeling the act of preservation as a gesture that alienates them from their surroundings. Another way they wouldn't talk would be to describe themselves as "idealists," but that's what they are— not, as they like to maintain, very "practical-minded" at all. Indeed they are preservationists too, but what they want to preserve is an idea, not a thing. They claim to remember, or at least to have inherited a memory of, a community that functioned organically, without the "artificial" interventions of people who would impose regulations, declare buildings or land inviolate. Of course, this is largely a myth, as a glance at the town's contentious history will tell you. We've been squabbling here continually for 250 years. But what matters is their belief in an unfettered past. There's an almost noble sort of cut-off-your-nose-to-spite-your-facedness about them. Even if their laissez-faire approach will now spell the destruction of the symbols of the old life, they would rather lose the symbols than what they think remains of the life itself. Philosophy underpins what often seems a cranky insistence on being left alone. The real town, in their eyes, is a place where people mind their own business, and if only by that definition, things work out all right.

We're brothers under the skin, these people and I. And we are both a bit addled. We are all antimodernists. They long for the return of a past informed by fierce independence. I long for a time of changeless surroundings. We both suffer from nostalgia, that fondness for something that never was.

4. Two American Places

A COUPLE OF YEARS AGO I went to Orlando, Florida, with my wife. More on a mission than a holiday, I went intending to "understand" Walt Disney World, suggesting a removed academic sort of stance, which, as things turned out, was hard to maintain.

We arrived in the middle of the night, and our first real experience of the park happened at breakfast in our hotel. In the restaurant foyer a large Minnie Mouse was posing with children—we had stumbled into what they call a "character breakfast." Goofy was wandering around, and when we had been seated he came by our table. We had a friendly wave for him. Next Chip stopped by. (Chip of Chip 'n' Dale?—I didn't remember, actually, but that's his name.) Chip decided to sit down on the banquette and he put his arm around my wife pantomiming, *I'm gonna steal your girl*. Reader, I could have behaved much, much better in this situation. Could have rubbed my eyes: boo hoo. Could have "put up my dukes."

Instead I smiled weakly. This was not an adequate response, and it left Chip, I now see, with little choice but to do what he did, which was to lean over my scrambled eggs and propose that we rub noses. *Still friends.* Here things went from bad to worse, because I'm afraid I said, still smiling my ghastly smile, the following sentence: "Thanks, old buddy, but I don't think we'll do noses today." We should have, though, because Chip still needed an exit strategy, which he found by tousling my hair and kissing me on the head. (This might have been a difficult moment had I been a younger man, and it is interesting to wonder what does happen when someone slugs Chip, but I had achieved a certain mellowness and it was all . . . fine.)

Soon enough I was walking about in the warm Florida winter air, and getting my first real glimpse of the scope of Disney World and experiencing a feeling I have had in many parts of the world, at the Great Pyramid, say, despite the presence of beggars, touts, and larcenous camel drivers (none of which were a problem at Disney World of course). It's a feeling everyone knows, not pleasure, really, but the tourist's sense of self-satisfaction: *By God, this really needs to be seen and I am seeing it.*

We were staying at a hotel called the Beach Club, which stands right next to the Yacht Club, both of these creations of the nostalgic postmodern architect Robert A. M. Stern, incorporating outsize emblems of New England seaside buildings: gray shingles, widow's walk, windmill. Of course they are not really beach or yacht clubs, at least insofar as such places imply membership, boats, an ocean, and so on. The only water nearby is an artificial lagoon, which is, though, equipped with a lighthouse. On the other side of the lagoon lies the BoardWalk complex, so it's as if you could stare across the "ocean" from Nantucket to Atlantic City. Other hotels loom behind, notably the huge Swan, with its giant rooftop statues of its namesake bird. The Magic Kingdom is out of sight, but you know it's there. Disney World occupies forty-seven square miles, and yet in its sameness one feels quite contained, as if by an invisible fence; indeed one feels somewhat claustrophobic.

We set out to tour the famous Epcot, which has a "World Showcase," a series of representations of various countries around the world. These resemble movie sets but they're more substantial, containing shops and restaurants. We started out at the United Kingdom, with its convincing and quite alluring Rose & Crown Pub, back to which I wanted to get for most of the rest of the tour. But Epcot is big, and when it was time for lunch we had fetched up on China's shores, only halfway around, having already seen a quaint quarter of a French provincial town, a street in old Marrakesh, a Japanese pagoda, the Piazza San Marco, a German beer hall, and a place called simply "Outpost," which stands in for the entire Third World and contains artifacts of world trade, chiefly old Coca-Cola shipping cases. This, with grim appropriateness, was about the only place in the World Showcase where you couldn't find a meal.

I am not the first person to speak lightly of Epcot, and I was all set to find it highly amusing. But I did not. I found it strangely oppressive. It was as if Chip's hand remained on my head. Later, when we finally reached the Magic Kingdom, we took the classic ride "It's a Small World." This made explicit Epcot's real message.

The message is that the world is not small in the sense of sharing universal ideals or in the sense that we are all brothers and sisters—it is small as in diminutive, cute, and essentially dismissible. Everything in the world is a cartoon—everything, that is, except us. Reality is reserved for those of us walking around, the big, well-fed people, the Americans. (Lately the world has begun to repay this joke. Disney World seems to attract a disproportionate number of the *very* well fed, the American obese, and foreign tourists often report that the thing they like to do most at the park is to "look at all the fat people.")

Walt Disney is what America had—and, please don't misunderstand, this is really a patriotic idea—Walt Disney is what we had instead of Hitler. He gave us a fascism of smarm. If real fascism ever comes to this country, can one doubt what it will look like? It will not be goose-stepping legions and blaring music. It will be cute, like a Disney movie. There will be country music and laconic heroes and lovable dogs. The second presidential campaign of George W. Bush perhaps gave just a hint of what it would be like. (Just as his governance gave us a foretaste of how the Constitution could be simplified.)

Disney World is like America now in certain ways: It is like us in its love of broad sentiment and bright colors and violent movement—it has helped to teach us those things. It is like America in its celebration of democracy—that is, an aspect of democracy: democracy as leveler, enemy of pretension. And it's like America when, as is so often the case, one place proves disappointing: you think that the best must lie ahead, and you move on. But it is not America, as I could tell by the way I felt when I crossed the park's borders back to the real thing. Would "free" be too strong a word?

About the same time I visited Las Vegas. I'd been there before and for some reason sort of liked it, and on the way in from the airport by cab, approaching the garish lights of the city, I began to get quite cheerful. I am not a compulsive or even a very enthusiastic gambler, and I was not looking forward to anything in particular, and yet my mood continued to lighten.

I was staying at Luxor, the world's third-largest hotel. This was not quite the distinction it might seem in Las Vegas, inasmuch as eight of the hotels on the world's top-ten list can be found along the Strip. Luxor was hard to miss: the black glass pyramid with the 120-foot obelisk in front. At night a bright light shone from the hotel's peak, in imitation, I guess, of the eye in the pyramid on a dollar bill. I arrived at night but the next day took a tour of the Strip. Luxor was close to the south end of the Strip, and walking north I passed by Excalibur, built on a Knights of the Round Table theme, to go directly to New York–New York, its half-scale Statue of Liberty rising from its rendition of New York harbor, which includes a tugboat and a fireboat and a skyline: the Chrysler Building, the Empire State Building, and CBS's Black Rock. Around the corner a bit of the Brooklyn Bridge ornaments the streetside façade.

Architectural collage had at that moment emerged as the characteristic genre of Las Vegas construction. Bellagio had created an eight-acre lake for its entrance, meant to suggest Lake Como. Paris, across the street, featured a Louvre-like façade merged with that of the Palais Garnier, the whole thing surmounted by an Eiffel Tower whose hind legs actually rested indoors, in the middle of the casino. An Arc de Triomphe (at two-thirds the size of the original) dominated the hotel's courtyard. The Eiffel Tower stood only half as tall as the real thing, but like a half-scale Statue of Liberty, it was no small structure. The whole of the Paris casino, with bistros and kiosks, lay beneath a false sky intended to simulate a Parisian twilight.

As I soon discovered, halfway down the Strip at the Venetian, the twilight sky provided another leitmotif in Las

Vegas architecture. The Venetian, which had taken verisimilitude to new ecstasies of detail with the faux-Baroque columns and "faithful reproductions" of works by Titian and Veronese in its lobby—also had constructed on its shopping mezzanine a version of the Grand Canal (here verisimilitude breaks down), with gondoliers plying their trade from store to store. As at Paris, the light told you it was about nine o'clock on a spring evening.

The exuberance of this fakery has its detractors, and I would have thought they would include me, though I found myself enjoying it. Some say that these settings offer a "sanitized" version of experience—the romance of Venice without the crowds or the stench or the language barrier. But I can't believe that people really believe they're having a New York or a Venetian or a Parisian experience in Las Vegas. We like this architecture, if we do, for its ingenuity, not its realism. We're gratified that someone has gone to such lengths to entertain us: it's performance architecture. (And it's nearly as impermanent as performance; hotels rise and fall all the time.)

Why doesn't this stuff have the same oppressive effect that Disney World has? After all, a greedy corporate mentality surely runs this place too. But somehow it's all different. Perhaps the Disney World architecture is such an affront because it is so prettified and the things it imitates are more vulnerable to parody. The New England seacoast motif at my hotel, with its exaggerations and false notes, was stylized in a way that seemed to diminish the real place, a place close to my heart. I love Venice too, but Venice can take it. Venice is impervious to this sort of assault in a way that Damariscotta, Maine, is not. The everyday scenes from around the world at Epcot—you know you shouldn't get upset at these things, but (at least if you're as thin-skinned as I am) you do. The big difference, though, between these two American places—both of them, let's face it, grotesque—is this: Las Vegas just wants your money. Disney World wants more than that; it wants your belief. It is trying to wish a vision of the world on you and the vision is cute and friendly but it doesn't feel that way. It feels menacing.

Las Vegas provided me a strange kind of comfort, a sense of being at home. At the luxury hotel Bellagio, the "lake" each evening offers a sequence of water shows—thanks to 40 million dollars' worth of fountains, jets of water spray up 460 feet into the air. I watched one that was choreographed to a part of *Appalachian Spring*. The jets rose and fell in perfect consonance with the swelling music, and in a little interlude just before the Shaker theme is repeated, the sprays dissolved into a cloud of mist. Then, as the stately finale began, the water erupted. Boom! A new fountain arose. Hearing this music I can never keep the words out of my head and there they were again. "'Tis the gift to be simple"—the water shot up on every beat—"'Tis the gift to be free." From the bar where I was sitting you could look across the "lake" at "Paris." At that moment, I could not recall having felt before such an emphatic sense of being where I belonged: in America.

And so we bid farewell to Las Vegas, happy enough to have been there and to leave. After I returned I was asked about the trip by a friend and I said, "Well, it was fun, though I think it would have been less fun if I hadn't been writing about it."

He brought me up short by saying, "Isn't everybody writing about it?" I was annoyed by the remark at the time, but as I thought about it I saw his point. Las Vegas provides one of the pleasures that more elevated travel sometimes fails to provide: it asks for a response. No one wastes any time looking for the "real" Las Vegas and no one feels intimidated by the culture it represents. It is the essential American place; but, perhaps, as a giant piece of installation art, a gloss on the country, it is not a place at all.

In its riot of decontextualization, in its relentless fraudulence, it parodies all those qualities of American—increasingly of Western or modern—life that we find so trying. To be here is to be in a place that is unafraid of its worst self. It revels in disconnection and incoherence. It invites us to do the same, and thus provides a holiday from our effort to make sense of the places we are in. But then the holiday ends, and we realize afresh how much we want places that in themselves make sense.

5. My Mall

THE OTHER DAY I stopped at the Hampshire Mall, down in the valley, about twenty-five miles from where I live. The "valley" is the Pioneer Valley, a commercial name concocted a few decades ago to package, for the minds of visitors, a place that oughtn't to have needed such packaging, a place with considerable history and beauty. It is the valley that lay below Thomas Cole in 1836 as he did his painting *The Oxbow*. The valley then was felt to be one of the country's scenic wonders, and people came from some distance to ascend the little mountain at its southern end and replicate the view that Cole had painted. Farms dotted the broad, flat meadows between the Connecticut River and the hills. The road that crosses the valley, between the towns of Amherst and Northampton, carried Emily Dickinson's carriage. (As we know from her letters, she went to Northampton at least once before her reclusive years began, to see Jenny Lind, "The Swedish Nightingale," perform. The poet drolly referred to the singer's "curious trills.") Amherst College was well established by then, and driving east one could see its high square bell tower above the trees.

The valley has not fared entirely well in recent years. Now strip development lines the road. A Target store, Dick's Sporting Goods, Whole Foods, the Cinemark—these are the main features of my mall, but strung out along the road are also a Trader Joe's, and a place called Dave's Soda and Pet City, chain restaurants, gas stations, car washes, and motels. If you catch it at the right angle you can frame the white bell tower of the college between the golden arches.

Agriculture has not left the valley, and indeed the mall abuts a farm. Seen from the highway the farm's twin blue silos float above the Cinemark, and all along the road, commerce backs up onto pastures and hayfields. Despite the particular provenance of the scene, it is not now an unusual landscape—one might almost say it is typical of the collision of symbols at the edge of the countryside in fields all across the country.

One of the troubles with "strip" development is that, although everyone deplores it, the language of our disapproval is exhausted. When you lament such a scene, you feel stale, tedious, cranky.

There is an academic discipline that ought to be able to help us in these situations: "cultural geography." It began in the 1920s, with the work of a Berkeley professor named Carl Sauer, who tried to turn the conventional study of geography on its head. Geographers prior to Sauer had taken as their subject the effect that land has on people. The Fertile Crescent gave rise to agriculture, the desert to nomads, the savannah to hunters, and so on. All very reasonable, indeed indisputable. Sauer pointed out, however, that it is often more interesting to look at things from another perspective, to study the way people change land—and in those changes one may reach a way of understanding the power and the politics that produced them.

I try now to apply the lesson of cultural geography to the mall and the farm, but it is confusing. The story is hard to read—it seems not so much politics as the absence of politics that explains strip development and sprawl. What record of conflict is left in this scene? One could read it as the forces of Big Business marching on the Small Farmer, and a passerby could easily animate this scene as a relentless war with a certain outcome, barns and silos falling before the onslaught of the bulldozer. As it happens, though, the scene, for all its visual discord, may be more static than it appears. Here politics do enter: the state has wisely been trying to protect agriculture and has bought up development rights from many farms to help them continue to operate. Some farmers have chosen to sell out to the developers, but presumably they have been rewarded. And, really, who has suffered economically? A farmer sold the land and made money. A developer built the mall and he made money. Store owners and franchise holders now run the businesses and they make money. Now people come to the mall. The money is flowing away from them, it is true, but no one is compelling them to be there. Are they suffering from "false consciousness"? Maybe, but only Karl Marx has ever been able to make that judgment with full confidence.

In the vacant eyes of that girl outside the Cinemark, the one with the studded nose and the low-riding pants, the one who probably slipped into the ladies' room to change into clothes her mother wouldn't let her wear—I suspect that in her eyes lurks a more sophisticated way of seeing the mall than in mine. She does not deplore it, certainly. It does not seem strange to her, perhaps that's the important point. It may even make her happy, a place of escape, just as the Marriott up the road is a place of escape for the illicit lovers, who find comfort in the very non-ness of place.

And, to be honest, I may occasionally be happy here too, if I find what I came to buy, and buy it, anonymously. You do not like to meet someone you know, someone who has any personal claims on you, at the mall. At the mall, we are relieved from what we profess to love—relieved from enacting a "sense of community"—so unlike Main Street, where the shopkeeper knows you and you are compelled to pause and chat, and feel bad if he doesn't have what you want and maybe buy something anyway to be friendly. If there is joy at the mall it is antisocial joy. Perhaps that's what we remember from the side of the road as we lament the "despoliation" of the landscape. We see a side of ourselves that we do not like. It is little wonder that when a crazed gunman wants to fire upon strangers he so often goes to a mall; in the mall his targets are dead to the imagination before they are killed, riding up and down the escalator like ducks in a shooting gallery.

No one has been exploited in the building of the mall. Yet something unfortunate has happened here. You can feel it. As you drive past, the scene is not uplifting. No one has been exploited, but everyone has. This is the feeling, of course, that exudes from much of built America, from our endless date-raped landscapes. Something that began as consensual has ended in tears.

6. Refuge

WE LEFT TOO LATE in the day and were utterly ill-equipped. We carried a blanket roll because we didn't own sleeping bags and because I had some notion, derived from westerns, that that was the right way to travel in the West. We hiked into a long trail in the Sierra Nevada, but only got two or three miles before darkness set in and we made camp "under the stars." We had a frying pan too, and some canned goods. We must have been carrying sixty pounds apiece. Happily, we were young.

And newly and hastily married, still in graduate school, penniless, without a plan. I had looked at the future and found it terrifying. Then we did what was in retrospect a natural thing: we walked into the wilderness. The second day, moving only a few score yards at a time in the thin air under our grotesque loads, we ascended above the tree line and gazed out on the Sierra peaks. Whatever our aim was, it worked. I had been relocated in the world—in a feeling I would experience many more times in life, both reduced by my place in the landscape and exalted. We hiked for two days and came back wanting nothing more complicated than lettuce.

As Leo Marx points out in his classic work of criticism *The Machine in the Garden*, America from its beginning has been riven by two opposing views of nature. On the one hand it is the "hideous wilderness" described by William Bradford in his *Of Plimouth Plantation*. On the other hand it is a paradisial land of bounty and beauty, The New World. As a practical matter we have solved this dilemma by having it both ways. We venerate nature and we tear it to pieces. It seems safe to say that no other society has so idealized nature while at the same time inventing so many ways to control and to destroy it.

In our literature, the wilderness has served as the last refuge. If there is an essential American plot it is "Boy meets woods." It is a flight from the falsities of society to the unquestionable truth of nature. Huck to "the territory," Ishmael to sea, Nick Adams to a campsite on the Upper Peninsula. As Leslie Fiedler pointed out years ago, this flight often represents an escape not only from society but more specifically from women. We needn't get into that debate to acknowledge that nature—uncivilized nature, wilderness—represents in our imagination the ultimate reality, and the ultimate escape from counterfeit reality.

What is wilderness? It seems an easy enough question. As

with the countryside, the answer is largely a matter of absences. A wilderness is a place where certain things have not happened. Like our literary heroes who take to the woods for freedom, we take to the woods to complete ourselves, to make ourselves whole. At some point, if you go far enough from roads, from buildings, from any human settlement, you declare yourselves to be having a "wilderness experience." Of course if you allow yourself to dwell on the problem it becomes more complicated. Wilderness experience is sometimes—to a certain extent it is always—made possible by wonders of human technology. Most people balk at driving motorized vehicles into "pristine" regions, but many consider it perfectly acceptable to be flown there. Moreover, even if one is traveling on foot, the lightweight gear now required for wilderness travel—the titanium alloys, the synthetic fibers, the freeze-dried foods—benefits from "space age" technology. And in the past few years a new element has been added: wireless communication. Now it is quite possible to be canoeing in the Adirondacks and to have your telephone ring. For that matter, you could be atop Mount Everest and still be in touch. It was one of the most unsettling elements of the terrible climbing tragedy that happened on Everest in 1996 that one of the doomed climbers was able to call his wife on a satellite phone as he awaited death. It made the whole event seem somehow stylized, not the epochal man-against-nature drama that in one way it truly was, but a game that just happened to turn deadly.

So there are little anomalies. But none of them really alters the essential dichotomy that seems hardwired into our culture: civilization versus wilderness. Even more than the distinction between the country and the city, the distinction seems God-given. What did I feel the first time I walked in the Sierra Nevada? It was a sense that I had left civilization, and therefore was exonerated from my civilized crimes: blunders and shortcomings and guilts and shames fell away. For a secular mind, "wilderness" has a nearly baptismal power to cleanse.

When I was there I was scarcely aware of a truth that, on later such trips, came actually to trouble me: my surroundings seemed wild but I was in fact in something that had been designated "wild." I was, really, in a park, and parks are not natural, they are man-made. Interestingly, this did not trouble those who created the first national parks, because they were (perhaps presciently) less interested in saving wildness than in showcasing beauty. Yellowstone was preserved exactly because its open plains and its geysers were not wild but parklike. No less an artificer of nature than Frederick Law Olmsted, creator of Central Park, was instrumental in the establishment of Yosemite and designed its roadways for maximum aesthetic effect. Certainly any traveler to one of the monumental parks would be better off now keeping his eye on the distant mountainside. The foreground is apt to be anything but aesthetically pleasing, with a crowded campground/parking lot of RVs with DVDs showing on screens within.

Recently a few writers have been questioning the whole idea of "wilderness"—most prominently, the ecologist and historian William Cronon. In his book *Changes in the Land* (1983), Cronon recounts the pre-Colonial history of the New England landscape. We have all inherited a myth about this place—land of the Pilgrims' pride—and according to the myth, just 450 years ago New England was an unmolested wilderness, whose indigenous people lived lightly on the land, hunting and fishing, essentially a part of nature themselves. Cronon quietly demolishes this notion. In fact, he points out, much of the land in New England was thoroughly managed by its Indian inhabitants. They ran the place as a sort of giant plantation and game preserve. They cleared broad fields on the coastal plain for agriculture, and burned the underbrush out of the inland forests to improve hunting. Tribal life of course did not accord with European models of settlement, and thus the colonists found no towns or private landholdings, no farms in the English sense of the word. (And the Indian population was already in decline, thanks to exotic diseases imported courtesy of the early explorers.) But the Indians' dominance of their environment was no less complete for all of that.

Cronon has gone on to broaden his inquiry into the elusiveness of the meaning of wilderness. For one thing, what was true of New England was true in various ways all over the country: from time out of mind, much more of the land than we have allowed has been altered by human habitation. (In the West, there was an additional irony: the land that was preserved in national parks as untouched wilderness had in many cases only recently become empty by virtue of the forcible removal of its Indian inhabitants.)

Charles Mann, in his book *1491*, has extended this view of New England to the whole of the New World. Drawing on the work of various anthropologists and historians, he has given us a startling view of an extensive Indian civilization predating the European encounter. It was a world more populous than Europe containing civilizations that were "swept away by disease and subjugation." "So thorough was the erasure," Mann writes, "that within a few generations neither conqueror nor conquered knew that this world had existed." To take just one example, the Amazon rain forest—symbol for environmentalists everywhere—is in fact not a virgin survivor from primordial time but an artifact of civilization. It appears that the Amazon supported an accomplished pre-Columbian population, far larger than currently exists, which had developed a sustainable way to grow crops on this notoriously fragile soil.

But perhaps more important than evidence of previous civilizations in what we take to be "virgin" areas is the evidence of our own shifting attitudes toward the wilderness. It, too, is land that has been altered not only by human intervention but by human perception as well. William Cronon built on his own insights about New England in his 1995 book *Uncommon Ground*. He writes, "The time has come to rethink wilderness. . . . The more one knows of its peculiar history, the more one realizes that wilderness is not quite what it seems. Far from being the one place on earth that stands apart from humanity, it is quite profoundly a human creation—indeed, the creation of very particular human cultures at very particular moments in human history." Wordsworth and the Industrial Revolution were required for the Alps to turn from monstrous to majestic. The wilderness has been variously an emblem of our fears and hopes, a ready metaphor for everything savage that civilization is meant to overcome, and a lost paradise.

At our current moment of history, dependent as we are on technology, and successful as we have been in dominating the natural world, the "wilderness" has come increasingly to be seen as a benign and beloved place. Nature itself has always been a gold standard for human ideas, the ultimate reference point—and, of course, depending on one's mood or philosophical predispositions, one could find verification in nature for just about anything. Hobbes could peer into the woods and see the base savagery of the human condition; Rousseau could look into his woods and see naught but innocence. But in the last century, especially in recent decades, nature has become something more than a textbook from which to learn about ourselves. It has become the repository of a virtue that eludes us. It has become a widely accepted notion, for instance, that nature left to its own devices is self-regulating, in effect a form of government superior to any we have devised, a sort of leaderless utopia. (Interestingly, the new breed of botanists and biologists has challenged this most cherished of popular ideas too, and the evidence suggests that the "balance of nature" is really a myth—populations of plants and animals often swing wildly out of control even without human tampering.)

Once, for a shining moment in the early days of the republic, we had a view of nature with human beings securely in their place. Nature and human life are continuous in Emerson's fine view: nature is the measure and source of all things, including the human mind and spirit; the machine no less than the flower is a product of nature; all truth can be found at its core. Emerson writes of the "moral sentiment which thus scents the air, grows in the grain, and impregnates the waters of the world, is caught by man and sinks into his soul." Imagine feeling that. It's gone, though it is hard to think that we do not all yearn for exactly this sense of order and connection.

In the tradition of American "nature writing" that grew up in the mid-to-late nineteenth century, Emerson's unity has already fled. Civilization and its misdeeds become the energizing force of much of this writing, from John Muir to Aldo Leopold and beyond. I suppose we can lay it all at the humble doorstep of Thoreau's cabin, though that seems grossly unfair because of the wit and spaciousness of *Walden.* Thoreau was never really writing about nature but about life. Nonetheless all are his followers and all seem to remember only the opposition of the natural world and society. In Leopold's classic *A Sand County Almanac,* for instance, the premise is announced at the start: "Now we face the question whether a still higher 'standard of living' is worth its cost in things natural, wild, and free."

Writing in this genre can be good and bad, and at its best it often gives us a fineness of observation and sometimes rises to lyrical heights, but all the thought seems to have happened before, and it is not very intricate thought at that.

There is a practical problem in our veneration of uncorrupted nature. We dismiss the places where our actions might affect the world for the better. "Idealizing a distant wilderness too often means not idealizing the environment in which we actually live, the landscape that for better or worse we call home," says William Cronon, and he is right. Late one afternoon toward the end of winter in 2007 I took the road that winds through the mountain passes of the Great Smoky Mountains National Park, in Tennessee. It's scarcely a "wilderness experience" (you're in a car on a wonderfully designed road with abundant turnoffs for the view). But especially at twilight on an early springlike day, it has a beauty both majestic and serene, patches of snow on the ground and the first stirrings of green on the mountainside. Night falls. Then you emerge from the park directly into the

town of Gatlinburg and it is a bubble of neon, like a miniature Las Vegas. Gatlinburg, a town of just 3,500, has accom-
modations for 35,000 visitors (provided apparently by a
branch of every motel chain known to man) and it has such
street attractions as the Guinness World Records Museum.
The contrast between town and park is grotesque and yet the
two entities make such a symmetrical pair as to be kind of
spellbinding. I found myself wondering what a child
brought up in contemporary America, accustomed to the
unruly tangle of strip-mall commerce, might make of it all,
and it occurred to me that such a child might be honestly
confused: What is natural and what artificial, what is
wild and what tame? The beautifully cared-for national
park seemed so controlled, so managed, and the town as
chaotic and self-generating as . . . well, as nature. Gatlinburg
seemed, right before my eyes, to enact the dark vision the en-
vironmentalist Alston Chase evokes when he imagines a
world of the not very remote future in which the only nature
that remains lies protected in national parks, with the fast-
food and souvenir emporia built right up to the borders. It
is a gloomy endeavor: to "protect" nature by fencing it in.
To define nature as that which is nobly apart from us is
ultimately to condemn our very lives as a useless inconven-
ience to the world. Then again, as global warming seeped
into public awareness, that was an idea that seemed suddenly plausible. Many people of sensitivity began to feel that

self-rebuke was the only seemly attitude available to our entire species.

Some years ago, an assignment took me to Bikini Atoll in the South Pacific. The island has never been reinhabited since the hydrogen bomb testing in the 1950s for fear the persistent low-level radiation would be dangerous over the long term. Instead there was an effort under way to open the lagoon as a haven for scuba divers because of the ships that had been sunk there as part of the test. I don't know whether anything came of this, or whether there is ever a chance that the islanders or their descendants will return. I know how I felt being there. There was a solemnity about the place. It is stunningly beautiful. Giant rollers crashed against the outer beach of the atoll just a few yards away from the tranquil, protected waters of the lagoon. The lagoon was teeming with the various species of fish that had once sustained the small population. I was on a boat with some natives returning for a brief visit, and with a hand line they hauled a yellowfin tuna out of the water and carved it up and ate it on the afterdeck of the boat. But even if the fish and the breadfruit trees could once again provide a life, there was something about the atoll that made me think it never would, and never should be occupied again. It was, if in a demonic way, a sacred place. The awful explosion could never be forgotten. Human beings, having shown what they were capable of, would never be welcome here again.

There are a few other places like Bikini around the world, places such as the DMZ between North and South Korea that human beings have abandoned and that nature has "reclaimed." Such places fascinate the journalist Alan Weisman, who, in 2007, published a book called *The World Without Us*. It asked the reader to imagine the sudden extinction of the human race, and held out the prospect of a planet revolving on in our absence. How long would it take our great monuments to vanish? Not as long as you might think, was Weisman's invariable answer. Water would fill the subway tunnels of New York within days and begin to undermine the streets, which soon would heave and buckle. Lexington Avenue would become a river. The doomed streets would soon sprout grass and then trees that would hurry their destruction. Suburban houses, their roofs untended, would fall victim to water and rot within decades. Buildings of cement and steel would take longer of course, but eventually they too would crumble as their pipes repeatedly froze and tore apart walls and floors. Lightning strikes and widespread fire would be a certainty. After such ravages the city would effectively vanish. The human artifact that would survive longest would be our plastic accomplishments: bottles and toys washing up against the faraway ocean beaches, enduring perhaps for hundreds of thousands of years, until eventually evolution did its work and microbes appeared that could eat them. The book, as Weisman repeatedly pointed out, was written as a warning and a call to action. But no one could deny the strange excitement of its doomsday scenario. Cormac McCarthy's novel *The Road* depicted a world following an unspecified apocalypse with roaming bands of savages occupying the ruins, and it somehow warmed the popular heart and won a Pulitzer Prize. In this same strange, self-hating season of cultural history, movies—*Resident Evil: Extinction* and *I Am Legend*—similarly dramatized the fantasy of a vanishing human race. It was a prospect for which audiences proved to have a lively appetite, a taste that would have seemed quite strange in an earlier age.

It will be interesting for future generations—assuming, as I cheerily do, that we are not in fact actually exterminating human life on earth—to apprehend the change in perception of nature that began in the late years of the twentieth century, as the prospect of climate change became a generally accepted fact. One of the earliest prophets of the looming catastrophe was Bill McKibben, whose despairing view represented itself in the title of his book *The End of Nature*. Crucially, the "end" that McKibben foresaw was not a literal end of life on the planet. It was the end of an idea. "The idea of nature," he wrote, "will not survive the new global pollution. . . . By changing the weather, we make every spot on earth man-made and artificial. We have deprived nature of its independence, and that is fatal to its meaning. Nature's independence *is* its meaning; without it there is nothing but us." McKibben takes this concept to almost comic extremes:

"This new summer will retain some of its relative characteristics [i.e., it will be hot, crops will grow] . . . but it will not be summer, just as even the best prosthesis is not a leg."

One knows the feeling he describes, regret that the vast impersonal force of nature could somehow be humbled. But after all, it's not clear in what way it ever made sense to think of a separation between "us" and "it." Something less than 17 percent of the world's surface has escaped the direct influence of human beings. (As we don't now need McKibben to remind us, that "direct" is a considerable hedge: acid rain falls on the virgin lake, full many a desert flower is born to wither unseen in the heat of climate change.) It is nice to think that the percentage will not drop to zero. Inasmuch as we were inevitably dependent on nature, though, could nature ever be fully independent of us? Weren't we always destined to meddle and in some sense control? And there is something finally circular about the whole proposition. It is the ultimate version of the paradox about the noise of the tree falling in the empty woods: nature would not be "independent"—or beautiful, for that matter—without us to think it so. What does "the environment" mean except "that which surrounds *us*?" McKibben himself has an inescapably anthropocentric view: nature will find a way to survive, but it is our perceptions that will be mortally wounded.

The radical French philosopher Bruno Latour would be impatient with any dithering over this issue. He argues that the very concept of nature is itself a misleading construct, it demeans what it pretends to glorify, and it deserves a dire fate. "When the most frenetic of the ecologists cry out, quaking: 'Nature is going to Die,' they do not know how right they are. Thank God, nature is going to die. Yes, the great Pan is dead. After the death of God and the death of man, nature, too, had to give up the ghost. It was time; we were about to be unable to engage in politics any more at all." This may sound ironic, but it is not—only, perhaps, extravagant. (Latour, after all, is French, and the French hold politics in higher esteem than we do.) His argument (in *Politics of Nature*) is with those "political ecologists" who, in their insistence that nature deserves standing in all political discourse, would nonetheless denigrate nature by compartmentalizing it. At least I think that is a fair summary of Latour's basic stance—and insofar as it is, I am rather on his side. (I think Emerson would be too.) But it is hard to know for sure, because his prose is both dense and rich in idiosyncratic usages, and his goals utopian. His term for the politics he imagines, borrowed from the ancient left, is the "collective," and he explains in a glossary that it "refers to . . . a procedure for collecting associations of humans and non-humans." One imagines a small voting bloc of you and me, a giraffe, and a live oak tree. It is a project that will require work.

In any case, there is that ever-looming doomsday in which the separateness of nature would be forced upon us.

In the event of wholesale and cataclysmic change, our view of nature might, curiously enough, come closer to what it historically was: that is, we would experience a renewed awe—not the cozy admiration of "nature's wrath" that we enjoy in a televised hurricane but a true awe, unto terror. We would not be wistful for the old "Mother Nature," we would be frightened of what she had become, and we would cease to use sappy pronouns altogether. "She" would be "It." The return of the wilderness! The ground I stand on once was covered by a glacier. It could be again. The most dire of the environmental seers suggest a sudden change from warming of the northern hemisphere to abrupt freezing, as the Gulf Stream gets diffused by icemelt in the Arctic Ocean. Could it happen? So far global warming, if that's what it is, seems to have been mild, pleasantly disconcerting around here, more boon than tragedy: a longer growing season, later frosts in fall. Are the foliage colors dulled? Could be, but we will survive. But I look at the crest of the hill and imagine the glacier's first appearance there and then its relentless progress toward my "old" house, whose age would suddenly be an absurdist joke in geologic time as the little dwelling was crunched beneath the wall of ice. Such futurist fantasies function like pornography now, of course, but if these things actually happened, if Scotland froze over or if Manhattan flooded one day, would we not be suddenly thrust back into the terrified wonder of primitive human life? Except, I suppose, that it would be a wonder complicated by collective guilt, a remorse of a dimension not yet known on an earth that has had plenty already to feel remorseful about.

Meanwhile we live in the world that has been given to us. I happen now to be back in the "perfect place" I mentioned some pages ago, in southwestern France. It's harvesttime. The vines are heavy with grapes, and now comes the picking machine, which rolls through the vineyard astride the vines, shaking loose the grapes and scooping them up only to spew them out into a waiting stainless-steel cart at the end of the row. The machine may seem incongruous among the vines, but of course there is really nothing "natural" in the scene at all. The vines themselves are the result of planting, grafting, pruning, and fertilizing. The human hand is everywhere in the valley, even on the far hillside where more vines sit next to a fallow but tilled field. Except for the line of trees in the valley, spared for that spot by the architects of the landscape, there is nothing that has been untouched. Yet "nature" is not complaining, seems indeed to be happy to play its part. One can only be grateful both to this ground and to the society that has used it well.

Even the evangelicals have learned to reread Genesis to interpret "dominion" over the earth as something more solemn and humble than the slash-and-burn tactics this passage has been used to justify in the past. The updated concept is "stewardship." True, this scarcely removes the threat. Human beings have run things—wars, business, romance—

with sometimes spectacular blundering. But do we have—have we ever had—a choice except to try? Until now American culture has been characterized by two opposing attitudes toward nature, rapacity and romance, and both keep us from the respectful intimacy that is needed. It is only through our efforts that we can repair the damage done not only to the world but to ourselves. We want a whole nature because we want whole selves, and we are scarcely unreasonable in this desire.

We feel dislocated in nature in part because we have not come to terms with our role, with engineering and with artifice, nor with our utter dependence on the given world. We may long for something pure, instinctive, organic, when we must instead face the truth that everything we touch is thereby "artificial." And not just face it but celebrate it, because to live out a close relationship with nature may be to restore the reverence that makes us feel complete. As Charles Mann points out, if we want to protect the world in its "natural" state, we will have to "create the world's largest gardens." And to value the gardens that have been created already, and those that have gone to seed.

I leave my house and walk across the road and into the woods. In a couple of hundred yards I am out of sight of buildings. I stop and lean against a tree next to the pool of a little stream. The woods are a tangle of rotten stumps and healthy trees, of fallen limbs and sprouting seedlings. This is a very untidy patch of nature. I have not tended to these woods, no one has, not in years. Once they were a pasture—a rusted strand of barbed wire can be seen embedded in a tree by the edge of the brook—and many times, over hundreds of years, they have been logged. It is quiet here, but every few minutes you can hear the swish of a car on the state highway, half a mile away. No one would call this wilderness, but at moments like this, just a couple of minutes' walk from the telephone, I value it more than the craggy view I saw from a mountain pass years ago. It is land that has been meddled with and will be meddled with again, but now, if briefly, is uncalled upon, at rest.

PART III

Weeping Nation

1. *The Greening*

I LOOKED NOT LONG AGO at a book unopened for many years, that landmark work of the seventies called *The Greening of America*. It promised to show "how the Youth Revolution is trying to make America livable." The essence of the "Youth Revolution" was honesty, naturalness, openness. The author, Charles Reich, a middle-aged Yale law professor, made an unlikely prophet. But this was a time—and how the book brings it back!—when intellectuals performed *explication du texte* on the lyrics of the Jefferson Airplane and willed themselves younger and freer as they donned bell-bottomed trousers and let the thinning locks flow. Reich was not a dabbler, one could say that for him. He had a comprehensive theory of history that culminated in the magic moment of the sixties. He posited stages of culture, a kind of ascent from the primordial: Consciousness I represented the law of the jungle, Consciousness II represented civilization and its discontents (alienation, anomie), and Consciousness III, the flowering of human potential for love and community, as enacted by the "flower children" of the late sixties. For Consciousness III people, "the world is a community. People all belong to the same family, whether they have met each other or not. It is as simple as that."

Consciousness III, as Reich conceives it, is more than an idyll, it is also an active rebellion against what has come before—against the corporate, bureaucratic state into which our civilization seems to have ossified. At one moment in the book, Reich laments all the things that are "missing altogether from our lives or present only in feeble imitation of their real quality," and it is a comprehensive list indeed, including "Adventure . . . Sex . . . Bravery . . . Magic and Mystery . . . Spontaneity . . . Seasons . . . Inner Life . . . Wholeness . . . Affection . . . Community," to name just a few. If this seems a little dire, Reich asks anyone who doubts it to "look at the faces of America. Stand at a commuter train station and see the blank, hollow, bitter faces."

It is (and was at the time) easy to make fun of this book, in all its lyrical grandiose innocence. And yet it had great appeal to readers, and maybe they were only hearing what one hears now, not the announcement of a new "consciousness" but something more like nostalgia, a yearning for an Eden of uncompromised feeling, a polity based on love. We may laugh at it, but if Reich was off about the imminent transformation of human nature, he was right about a widespread longing in the culture. It is an irony that his list of things-we-have-lost might well have served as a thematic agenda for the advertising of the decades that followed. On TV and in magazines, traditional images of prestige and glamour made room for images of authenticity. This beer (car, cruise line, running shoe) would demonstrate that you are not a "bitter hollow face," you thrum with life, you are in touch with yourself, are real. However—and crucially—the ads seemed to encourage the dark side of the new sensibility: people's interest in individual perfection rather than in bonding with their fellows, an interest in distinction, not community.

During the decades that followed the quick rise and fall of Consciousness III, the sort of community that flourished in the country was one not of national but group identity. In one way, this must be seen as no small achievement, because corners of society that previously felt themselves voiceless were at last able to speak up. But it was accompanied by a sense of atomization in the culture as a whole.

If pluralism were not an undoubted virtue, we would have to declare it one, just to keep more people from going mad. We may not have achieved tolerance or equality or classlessness, but in America at the start of the twenty-first century we have achieved pluralism of a sort, the pluralism of simple acknowledgment. Hmong immigrants, members of the Augusta National Golf Club, the local coven of

Wiccans, supermodels, the transgendered, militant seniors—so many groups, all with a claim on our imaginations, all asking to be recognized as real.

There are times when this pluralism seems like the best thing we have done, and maybe it is. Who can hear the roll call of names read on the anniversary of the World Trade Center attacks, with their mosaic of ethnic origins, or watch a televised swearing-in ceremony for new citizens, and not feel moved, filled with a justifiable patriotism. This is tinged, true, with a lesser emotion—the reason no doubt the eyes moisten—a love of self for subscribing to this creed by which we so imperfectly live.

To do our society's ideals justice, your heart should swell daily with a Whitmanesque love of others. My heart usually fails me. Somewhere not far beneath my surface lurks a monster of squeamishness, a figure better suited to nineteenth-century London, a dandy, to whom almost everyone in the vast empire is exotic, a curiosity. I recoil at every hand: from teenage loiterers, with their trousers pooling about their ankles, from corpulent coifed and bejeweled golden-agers, from squinty-eyed gents vain of their abs, from—well, from appalling legions of my fellow citizens.

This is a poor attitude for a Democrat, but I think I am not alone. David Brooks has put a happy face on the fragmentation of society by noting our tendency, faced with the overwhelming multiplicity, to retreat into little worlds of self-defined superiority. He calls this the "democratization of elitism." He writes, "Everybody gets to be an aristocrat now. You can be an outlaw-biker aristocrat, a corporate-real estate aristocrat, an X-Games aristocrat, a Pentecostal-minister aristocrat . . ."

Mark Penn, the political pollster, celebrates the fragmentation of society (the "niching of America") in his book *Microtrends,* published in 2007. Penn writes of the power of small groups: "It takes only 1% of people making a dedicated choice—contrary to the mainstream—to create a movement that can change the world." Some of Penn's niches seem less than world-changing: "Cougars," or women dating younger men, for instance. Some are rather interesting: "Impressionable Elites" who counterintuitively show more interest in political candidates' personalities than do less well-educated voters. But Penn revels in it all as the bloooming of a society of free choice—"There is no One America anymore, or Two, or Three, or Eight. In fact, there are hundreds of Americas, hundreds of new niches made up of people drawn together by common interests."

This was all very upbeat, and yet you feel the hollowness of parochial identities. And they obscure the great chasms in the country, notably the division of fortune. If the sheer size of the society has helped us to hive off into substantial little cultures, not all of them are benign. We have, justly, heard a lot about the most significant niche of all, the richest one percent of the population, which received at last count some 22 percent of the nation's income. (Entry level in annual income was about $350,000 in 2007, but the average income was closer to a million.) Meanwhile the bottom half of the population received just 13 percent of the national income. One percent of the country is 3 million people, a perfectly ample pool from which to draw your friends, indeed a little country within the country, the country of the rich. It was quite possible to live in the land of the one percent and to have little or no intimate contact with anyone outside it. Should you be a member of that truly rarefied slice of the wealth—the top tenth of one percent that commands 7.4 percent of the wealth—it was almost certain that the only people you would see outside your circle of peers would be functionaries of one kind or another. What was true at the top was true, perhaps even truer, at the bottom. Adrian Nicole LeBlanc, chronicler of the women of the South Bronx, reported that her subjects, tough and brazen as they were in their neighborhood, would not think of venturing into Midtown because of the intimidation they thought awaited them there.

Just as the contested nature of place makes no place seem real, so, too, the profusion of group identities seems to blur the reality of each, until we all—even, it is nice to think, the very fortunate—feel like costumed figures on a stage, subjects of a vast National Geographic television special. In that situation what the world needs is people who rise above the crowd—and in its cleverness and fecundity the world creates such people every day.

2. Celebrity

I DON'T DISLIKE CELEBRITIES. Our "celebrity culture" is much and properly lamented, but then again what would we do without these human landmarks, these symbols? They are called living legends for a reason. With their publicized exploits they provide the stories we otherwise, sitting around the fire in the cave watching the shadows on the wall, would have to invent. Thank God that there are people willing to trade their privacy and often their dignity for fame.

But if I don't dislike them, I do dislike being around them.

So I say. And so I think, but why am I waiting to meet the famous writer, humorist, and media presence KG?

This has been a perfectly pleasant evening so far—a reception for Miranda, after her poetry reading. An evening full of the stifled yearnings of provincial intellectual life, but nonetheless nice in its way—warm, comfortable.

Suddenly a ripple goes through the room: he's coming!

KG happens to be a friend of Miranda's, he's been performing at a college nearby, and he's been invited to drop in at the reception. He's called to say, yes, he's on his way.

I could leave, but don't, though part of me dreads meeting KG.

We sometimes speak of celebrity as if it were a binary system—the famous and the obscure—but of course it's a far more nuanced thing. Dominated as our culture is by its outsized personalities, nonetheless it takes a lot to unite the consciousness of 300 million people, not all of them operating at full alertness. At any one moment some 30 percent of the people can't name the vice president of the United States, for instance. One could probably define a sliding scale of celebrity that begins at entry level when a person is simply known by people he does not know, and ends in Beatlemania. At one end of the scale, there is honored Miranda herself—she could walk unrecognized through her own hometown, and yet in a hall of librarians and English professors she would be "known." As for KG, well, he is not a regular fixture on television, and thus his recognition level is measured in the tens of millions, not the hundreds of millions. But that's still a lot of wattage, considerably more than is usually found at a poet's reception.

KG arrives.

What's he like? Well, you know—he's just as he is onstage: wry and tart, self-deprecating and completely self-absorbed, perfectly charming. He dominates the room. KG is a paradigmatic American celebrity. He has achieved success by mocking his failure, he is famous for being obscure. He presents himself as a hapless outsider, a bumpkin, and his weaknesses are what we love about him. Still, anyone who thinks about it realizes that now he flies in the front of the plane, lives uptown, and gets good tables wherever he dines. So the more successful he becomes the more inaccurate his self-presentation becomes, even though his performance depends on what sounds convincingly like self-effacing candor. He's not unaware of the problem, one can tell, and he seasons his routine with references to things like, oh, Brie as a comic acknowledgment. It's quite a delicate thing, when you think about it. It would be interesting to talk about, of course, but as I say my hellos I can't imagine a way to introduce that topic that wouldn't sound—would not in fact be—hostile. ("Doesn't your life necessitate your being a fraud?")

In ones and twos we drift into and out of KG's orbit, murmuring praise, and a peculiar thing happens—or maybe not so peculiar, since it always seems to happen in situations like this. The event has changed tense. It seems to be occurring in the future perfect. Accepting the impenetrability of KG's persona, we realize that we are not here to meet him, we are here so that we will have met him. And so as we listen to him it is in our minds already tomorrow, and we are saying to someone, "Guess who was there—KG!"

With him, as with most celebrities, the encounter makes for a far better experience in retrospect than it could ever be in fact. As a memory—a retail-able memory—"knowing" a celebrity enlarges our sense of self. ("KG? Oh yes, I met him once, really a very nice guy, very human.") Often enough the meeting itself only serves to diminish us, stirring discontent, even self-contempt at our (generally insincere) deference, our complicity in a charade.

This is an unpleasant feeling. But there's an easy way to deal with it. Just turn on the person who made you feel this way—the poor celebrity. ("KG? Oh yes, I met him once. What an egomaniac!") Celebrities understand the dynamic full well. It's another reason—along with stalkers, pie-throwers, and people seeking donations—for them to be wary of anyone who is not at least as famous as they are. They have learned the hard way the dangers posed by us, the treacherous people in their thrall (on whom, sadly enough for them, they depend utterly for their good fortune).

Not easy, being a celebrity. But we sort of envy them, don't we?

"Of all Americans, only they are complete," says George W. S. Trow about celebrities. The remark occurs in his book *Within the Context of No Context*, a meditation on, among other things, the nature of public and private life. And of course it's a deeply ironic remark, meant to say more about sad ordinary yearnings than about the glory of fame. But it doesn't entirely disown its meaning, that we impute a deeper reality to celebrities than we grant ourselves. They are substantiated, validated by their fame.

That's one truth on the subject. But the other is its opposite: we sometimes suspect celebrities of lacking any real life at all, the very marrow sucked out of their existence by their fame. And they themselves, particularly the politicians among them, like to encourage this notion (though we suspect them of rank disingenuousness) by talking lovingly, even enviously, about "real people," "ordinary Americans," as if with longing for a land from which they have been tragically exiled.

Every now and then we discover some admirable "ordinary Americans" and as a reward we turn them into celebrities, often enough with tragic results. Think for instance of the nine Pennsylvania coal miners in 2002, who became famous for not drowning when they were trapped in a flooded mine shaft. Their endurance during the hours of suspense, and the heroic and successful effort to save them by drilling a precise hole to their location, "captivated the nation." The miners were instant television personages, won a book and movie contract from Disney. The lead rescuer, a surveyor who had drilled the lifesaving hole, was also given a share of the money—largely, it was said, to prevent him from selling his own story to a rival company. A year later most of the lives involved had turned to ashes. Fame had proved less rewarding than it was hoped. The miners' agent said, "The big endorsements have just not been there." (One wonders what exactly they might have been expected to endorse. Rubber boots?) The lucky rescuer inspired the envy of fellow rescuers, and incredibly enough he earned the resentment of the trapped miners too. Apparently feeling an outcast, he shot himself dead.

Perhaps fame is best left to the famous. They are different from you and me. They're so different that we can't really decide the basic question of whether we love celebrities or hate them. I suppose we love them for living for us; we hate them for implying thus that we are dead. Little wonder they are pursued by madmen.

I have been using a couple of terms more or less interchangeably—"celebrity" and "fame"—but some would insist on a distinction. Fame in this view grows organically from achievement, whereas celebrity is manufactured, dependent as much on image as accomplishment. In his book *Intimate Strangers* Richard Schickel says that while we have always had fame, celebrity is a relatively recent phenomenon. Indeed, there were no celebrities before the twentieth century, Schickel declares. One could quibble. The story of Buffalo Bill, who got rich by portraying himself in his Wild West shows, prefigures much that is loopy in our culture. But I see Schickel's general point. The distinction, though, begins to fade. It is easy to find examples on each side of the fence from a few decades ago—General Marshall was famous; General Patton was a celebrity. But celebrity has now become so all-encompassing that it eclipses and enfolds fame—with our hunger (and our sense of entitlement, our right to know everything) we celebrify those whom we might once have been content only to admire.

Schickel traces celebrity to the movies. He's persuasive: there, people were made literally larger than life by technology. And crucially their audiences began to be more interested in them than in the characters they portrayed, interested in their ongoing story at the expense of the story on the screen. That was what it meant to be a "star." What a curious word, "star." I realize I have never spoken it without implied quotation marks. To use it unironically is to participate in a willing self-abnegation.

Assassin and autograph hound represent the polar extremes of our aberrant attitudes toward celebrities. But even those of us who claim sanity fall victim to a spurious imaginative involvement with the famous. To know what Jennifer wears to bed, how Meryl furnishes her Connecticut house, what Julia's favorite dessert is is to know . . . what? Well, nothing, of course, but rare is the person who has not enjoyed such empty knowledge. Of which, of course, what Jennifer wears to bed is the most significant. So much of our curiosity about celebrities—the glamorous, but even the less so (Camilla!)—has to do with sex. They are somehow fair game for our most prurient interest, as if that's the deal they made to be famous. Our tabloid minds may be fueled only by voyeurism, but it's probably something less perverted if more disheartening: the desire to make a connection with the world that is certified to be real.

Of this desire, Richard Schickel takes a particularly dark view. Schickel suggests that celebrities offer us a delusory way to simplify experience, to organize reality. He argues moreover that a fascination with celebrity is nothing less than a "desperate hope that the cult of personality may substitute for a sense of organization, purpose, and stability in our society."

This strikes me as an overstatement. But there is little doubt that our minds get clouded on the question of celebrity, and if they do, I suspect it is because they are clouded about much more.

3. Unreal

DURING THE LATTER HALF of the twentieth century a notion, a conceit that once had been the province of artists, had come to belong to everyone—that notion was that the world is illusory, that all "reality" is subjective. Once, this was enough of a provocation to mock the bourgeoisie into discomfort and self-doubt. But then the bourgeoisie claimed the wisdom for their own. Through a mishmash of philosophy, popular art, and adulterated science (relativity, the Uncertainty Principle), and even the "drug culture," the unreliability of perception became commonplace. Everyman a Pirandello. The Beatles sang of it (nothing is real, nothing to get hung about) and people learned to exclaim with a roll of the eyes, "Unreal!"

In 1967, Jacques Derrida, then a name known to few, delivered a paper at Johns Hopkins University, "Structure, Sign, and Play in the Discourse of the Human Sciences."

The doctrine of deconstruction had arrived on our

shores. If it was largely inscrutable, that did not mute its effect. After all, difficulty often creates wealth in an intellectual doctrine, opening the way for a multitude of disciples to interpret and disseminate the word. Nor is internal contradiction a bad thing, either, and deconstruction encompassed a major paradox. On the one hand it taught that all language was to be distrusted; on the other, it suggested that everything was a text. There is no meaning outside of words, and yet words have no meaning, at least no "stable" meaning. It was a perfect doctrine for a subjective world.

There was a wisdom at the center of this doctrine, an understanding of the tautology that haunts all language. But the wisdom had been available before Derrida. In retrospect one can say about the deconstructionist movement—which has not ended but which nonetheless has taken a place in history—that whatever else it did it provided an enormous amount of fun for people. It was fun to practice, and fun to disparage.

There was, to be sure, a darker side to deconstruction. This case is perhaps best made by David Lehman in his book *Signs of the Times*. He argues that the theory is essentially nihilistic, and that the nihilism matters—or can, or should. "There is no ultimate meaning to which one can penetrate. There is only the constant deferral of meaning, the infinite play of signification." Lehman's objections are more than abstract. The book turns on the sinister story of Paul de Man, revered Yale English professor and deconstructionist critic. De Man, it turned out, had led another life in Nazi-run Belgium, where he was a collaborator and propagandist. Lehman argues convincingly that for de Man deconstruction was a theoretical justification of the erasure of his past, a vast amnesty project for his collaboration. By his calling into question the absolute truth of anything, the absolute truth of his crime was washed away. The de Man story, Lehman says, forced one to examine "two realms usually kept in separate compartments: the realm of literary theory and the realm of historical actuality."

If one took it seriously deconstruction could be very bad news. As one critic succinctly put it, "It cruelly reduces the world to words." But for most people who cared at all, it was not a tool of nihilism, just one of freedom. You didn't have to be a covert Nazi sympathizer to experience the liberation that deconstruction could bring. The notion that what other people held dear was simply a "construct" could relieve one of quite a bit of envy, longing, intimidation.

Of course, a strict adherence to the faith would have resulted in a world of chaos. But one could fudge. Even two deconstructionists can agree on what time to meet for lunch, and they will not worry overmuch about the meaning of "one o'clock" or what constitutes, really, lunch. Similarly, many of the things that *you* held dear could be exempted from deconstruction. So you could have had a pleasant life in the world of unexamined reality, but the freedom at any moment to call into question the validity of anything.

For the academic, deconstruction was a social leveler—no more deference to "the canon" or to those who, by virtue of their education and status, laid special claim to it. Little wonder that the tweed jackets tended to deplore deconstruction and the Levi's liked it. And ultimately to be "into theory" was a status enhancer too: you knew the lingo, you were in the club.

History had given us a joyous new way to be. It was skeptical unto paranoia, but a wholesome paranoia: it reveled in the disjunctions of the modern world. It was a kind of creative despair. It was postmodernism. It was great. But I think that for almost everyone, including those who reveled in it, it was not quite enough. Like so many other excursions into indeterminacy it was a flirtation with the enemy. "Theory" provided a way to be jaunty about something that was in fact a discomfort, an underlying unease about the nature of reality.

In 1999 the movie *The Matrix* appeared, a straightforward little story, if you could buy into its science fiction vision, which posited a futuristic world that was only imagining its own life. Most of its citizens lay comatose, their bodies warehoused, their brains connected to a vast computing network providing the illusion of experience. And (the clever part) it's a shared illusion, because the individual brain is linked to those of the other zombies of the world.

(Evil machines run the show, of course, and a few escapees oppose them, and thus we have a plot.)

It turns out that a small body of academic literature preceded the movie, an exploration of what is known as the brain-in-a-vat problem. It poses the question of whether you might actually prefer a life full of glory and passion and delight even though it was all a delusion and "you" were a disembodied brain receiving programmed stimuli.

I've got to say that the brain-in-a-vat problem holds limited interest for me, and *The Matrix* isn't my cup of tea, either; anything that's bathed in green light and involves the future makes me want a frothy comedy set somewhere like Saint-Tropez a few years back. But the movie had quite a following, and not just among sun-deprived, underweight young men, either. It seems to have tuned into a widespread anxiety. I don't mean that large numbers of people are worried about being vat-brains. But maybe they are worried about something for which *The Matrix*'s creators found a metaphor. Adam Gopnik, in *The New Yorker*, put the case simply: "The idea that the world we live in isn't real is one that speaks right now to a general condition." Gopnik went on to say, "The monopolization of information by vast corporations; the substitution of an agreed-on fiction, imposed from above, for anything that corresponds to our own reality; the sense that we have lost control not only of our fate but our small sense of what's real—all these things seem part of ordinary life now."

Is this true? If it is not true, it has at least become an acceptable observation. Gopnik's vision of an Orwellian corporate-consciousness machine might have seemed an extravagant remark not long ago, but who would bother to argue with it now? Well, a network executive would, and any number of people might have their quarrels, but it is the stuff of ordinary intelligent conversation.

Another movie came along at about the same time, *The Truman Show*, more entertaining, less ghoulish, but similar in its appeal to our misgivings about the reality of our world. *The Truman Show* imagined its hero to be the victim of a lifelong hoax: he thinks he's living a normal life but in fact he's the subject of a reality TV show, filmed in a bland Potemkin village, rather like Celebration, Florida, with a cast of hundreds of actors playing his neighbors. When, in his mounting unease, he tries to escape by crossing the man-made lake at the edge of town, he ultimately sails right into the painted sky.

The notion that we live in a world of manufactured illusion had gotten such currency by the start of the century that an essayist in *Harper's Magazine* could go so far as to provide a taxonomy of contemporary unreality. Sample: "Covertly unreal realistic: Hair in shampoo ads. More or less undetectable digital effects, of which there are more every day."

The author was Thomas de Zengotita, and his argument was more literal than that of *The Matrix*, but it amounted to the same lament: they are messing with our minds. He was not claiming coherent conspiracy exactly, but more nearly saying that we are reduced to stupefaction by the sheer stuff of contemporary culture, the tsunami of "information" that breaks over our heads. And that much of that information— data, imagery, secondhand experience, whatever it is—is in fact tricked up by those contemporary illusionists, the people and institutions who are increasingly seen as one undifferentiated force, "the media."

Furthermore, they do their work so cleverly and with such energy, de Zengotita argues, that "all the content on our information platforms converges on this theme: there is no important difference between fabrication and reality." The occasion for this essay is the aftermath of the September 11, 2001, attacks, and the writer's point was that even this event, so monstrous and overwhelming in its immediate effect, quickly became reduced for most people to a set of images. He writes that the attacks were an event "so enormous, so horrific, so stark that even the great blob of virtuality that is our public culture would be unable to absorb it. But it could. It has."

De Zengotita's ultimate subject is numbness, our self-protective reaction to a dim knowledge that multitudes of images and emotions are being zapped at us, that "our inner lives are now largely constituted by effects."

You have to admit that there's something to this—a lot to it, really. On the one hand, you say, people have been telling us what to think for a long time; before television there was radio, and what about those old newsreels at the movies? What were they if not efforts to govern our emotions, and arguably more systematic and intentional efforts than any CNN, for instance, is inclined to undertake?

Still, you don't have to have an impossibly long memory to recall a time when things seemed a lot different, when there was no CNN, no MSNBC or Fox, not to mention channels devoted to golf, cooking, money, sex . . . when there was no Internet and "virtual" meant "more or less." The fundamental difference, perhaps, was not between truth and lies, it was simply that less of the world was seen secondhand, less was mediated and "spun." Within the memory of some is a world that was understood primarily with our eyes or by words read on the page, which immediately invite the critical faculties that images tend to override. (Not that words on the page haven't become part of the problem, because there are so many of them, an explosion of language. A magazine serves every conceivable interest. The number of books published annually in the United States climbed to more than 150,000 by early in the century, so if you read two of them a week you would read less than a tenth of a percent of what was newly available, never mind all the books you hadn't read from years and centuries before.)

But bring on the media conglomerate CEO—he-or-she will tell you that we are in the midst of a glorious revolution, in which more people know so much more. And isn't it true that we are more aware of places, events, even ideas in some form or other than we used to be, and isn't that a good thing? The political theorist Thomas Frank writes sardonically of this sort of claim, "Since democracy means having more consumer choices, and information technology will vastly increase the power of our channel changers, hey, presto! More democracy!"

The trouble—or one trouble, anyway—is that it's possible to be aware of more and to know less. Less, that is, in the sense of knowledge that has history, context, depth, experience. The marvelous things people now know how to say! *Market's up, a lot of this is just short covering. We had him in Tora Bora and we lost him. In the long run it's not the deficit but the balance of trade. I want to maximize my omega-3 but I've got to eat lower on the food chain. The Turks will always be scared of the Kurds.*

This pseudo-knowledge is our gift from the paid chatterers who often themselves don't understand what they are saying. I don't mean that no one understands the trade deficit and that no one is an expert on Afghanistan, only that all of us some of the time, and most of us most of the time, borrow expertise and speak knowingly of subjects, some of which we had never heard of a few days ago, about events that happen in places we have never seen. There is probably a number, a percentage of our knowledge that is second-hand—let's call it 78—beyond which we begin to feel unmoored no matter how "accurate" the knowledge is.

Moreover, we may be deluded about the actual variety of what we are seeing and—especially—hearing. It is possible for the images to multiply, but the range of allowable thought to shrink. What can be shown and said on television has vastly expanded in one specific way: the personal, and especially the sexual. I wonder sometimes if the conservatives who rail against such language and image are not secretly laughing up their sleeves, as the networks move to the left on sex and to the right on everything else.

For Bill Moyers, the determination of allowable thought is nothing less than a conspiracy. "Virtually everything the average person sees or hears, outside of her own personal communications," he said in a recent speech, "is determined by the interests of private, unaccountable executives and investors whose primary goal is increasing profits and raising the company's share price."

Moyers, by his own account, has had the opportunity to confront this conspiracy of interests and feel its power directly. It's a more subtle thing for most news practitioners, less adventurous or less committed, a matter of absorbing the zeitgeist, until one knows instinctively what the outside limits of expression are. Moreover, there are infinite subtleties to the unwritten and for the most part unspoken rules of what can be said. The "mainstream," for all these years a cliché, is, if you think about it, an apt metaphor: the mainstream has on its sides countless backeddies, bayous, and wetlands for marginal and dissenting opinion, and as with a river, they relieve the possibility of flood.

Thomas Frank has written about what he calls the new "cultural miracle" that can somehow co-opt any opinion. "What we understand as 'dissent' does not subvert, does not challenge, does not even question the cultural faiths of Western business," he remarks. Corporate executives "are hipper than you can ever hope to be, because hip is their official ideology. . . . That's them waiting . . . to congratulate you on how outrageous your new style is, on how you shocked those prudes out there in the heartland."

A confession: I love my media. I love my television, neat packager of the world, so like in that way to its natural enemy, the book. "The media, more and more, are our community," Richard Schickel has said. I agree. It treats loneliness. I really miss my guy, Tom. I watched Tom anchoring the news for years. Now he's gone. Sad. It was Tom's face that made all the difference. I used to watch for the moments when he earned his money, the millions of dollars a year paid by a grateful network for just that right little look at the end of the show, the moue, the half-smile, the wince, or the ghost of a grimace. And what a narrow range of expression it was, like carving on a cameo! Grave or wry, puzzled or moved—all adjectives are only approximations of the emotion being conveyed, which always transcended the moment. What Tom said to me was: "Old pal, you and me, in this crazy world, at least we are solid. God only knows what they're going to do next, but us, we've got our feet on the ground." The new guy, Brian, hasn't quite got it yet, but he will, he will.

I know people who turn away in disdain from all television, won't have it in their house. This may be a good idea. As they never tire of telling you, it frees up their time for higher pursuits. But it also strikes me as a form of that most popular, indeed epidemic, disorder called denial. Television is the way we live now, and how can you hope to be in touch with your culture (broadly understood) without it?

We say that TV news is entertainment, and it is, and we like it that way. At the dizzying media-saturated start of the Iraq War, someone around here was overheard to say without irony, "I've got to go home and watch the war." I expect the same sentence was uttered in many places. There is so much news that you can't attend to it all, and you begin to select stories as if they were programs. *The New York Observer* a while back interviewed a number of prominent sorts, asking them what stories they just sort of skipped. "The latest space shuttle, the Columbia disaster," said Frank Rich of the *New York Times*. "I have to say I find it kind of embarrassing," said Ira Glass of public radio, "but I missed the entire Kosovo war."

And it's not just the television. Print is a spectacle of its own. In the spring of 2003 the *New York Times* flamboyantly fired a young reporter who had "betrayed" the paper by pretending to have interviewed people in person when he had spoken to them on the phone, and by borrowing or fabricating quotes. Bad stuff. But much of what he invented was trivial. He said the home of Pfc. Jessica Lynch (remember her and her "daring rescue"?) overlooked cattle and tobacco fields. In fact it overlooked no such things. But what did it matter? What—to anyone trying to understand the war—did Pfc. Lynch's story matter?

The aspect of this case that might have given the *Times* most pause is that few of the "victims" of its misrepresentation complained. They thought this was the way of the world. In this they were falsely sophisticated. Reporters do care about getting their facts right. But the ordinary reader knew what the *Times* didn't want to admit, that much of the "news" exists to divert rather than to inform. And it doesn't do to think of ourselves as victims. It is just as possible that we are collaborators.

Perhaps it is not just the *media's* presentation of "news" but the *news*, the actual events, that has become entertainment in our imaginations. That is the argument of Neal Gabler, in his book *Life the Movie*. The conventions of popular culture—specifically the conventions of film—Gabler says, have become the way in which we perceive public events.

It has long been a stylish thought that the movies have an unusual power over our minds. Years ago, at cinema's infancy, the French critic André Bazin suggested that the point of film was to achieve perfect replication of reality—he called this the "myth of total cinema." And others have said that the movies went one better, that what was on film somehow exceeded life. Andy Warhol said, "I always thought that I was more half-there than all-there—I always suspected that I was watching TV instead of living life. People sometimes say that the way things happen in the movies is ureal, but actually it's the way things happen to you in life that's unreal. The movies make emotions look so strong and real."

Neal Gabler would agree: We see the world and we see our own lives. We borrow gesture, create scene, and craft a character or, more frequently, we craft multiple characters for ourselves based on entertainment. "We live in a movie, dreaming of celebrity."

For some readers, this description will recall Walker Percy's novel *The Moviegoer*, published in 1961. (Gabler himself does not choose to recall it, perhaps because the novelist was all too prescient, too long ago.) The book's hero, Binx Bolling, is a young New Orleans stockbroker, prosperous, with an easy way with women, and yet adrift in a world that seems to him illusory. He finds solace in the movies, not as an escape, exactly, but because they seem to him more real than life. "I am attracted to movie stars," he says, "but not for the usual reasons. It is their peculiar reality which astounds me."

Binx tries to undergird his own tenuous identity by

imagining himself on the screen. "I think it over Gregory-Peckishly," he remarks. In what is no doubt the book's best-known passage, he marvels at the magical authority a place suddenly takes on if it has the good fortune to appear in a movie. "If he sees a movie which shows his very neighborhood," he says, "it becomes possible for him to live, for a time at least, as a person who is Somewhere and not Anywhere." He calls what the movies do "certifying," making things real.

Percy's wisdom, though, was not about the movies, it was about the spiritual malaise that kept Binx from human connection. And I must register some skepticism about the magic of film. Maybe this is because I don't really think a movie has had a lasting effect on me since the Saturday afternoon westerns taught me the essential lesson of plot: "Meanwhile, back at the ranch . . ." But in Gabler's view, we are all Moviegoers now. Entertainment provides the tropes by which we understand ourselves and the great public events of our time, and often enough those events are themselves the result of a theatrical imagination. Gabler writes that "entertainment . . . is arguably the most pervasive, powerful and ineluctable force of our time—a force so overwhelming that it has finally metastasized into life.

"Life," he goes on, "would be the biggest, most entertaining, most realistic movie of all, one that played twenty-four hours a day, 365 days a year, and featured a cast of billions." This is, like much of the book . . . what? A bit sweeping? Yet there may be a worthwhile observation at the core.

If we have learned how to construct the world ourselves as a species of entertainment, then the world is all too eager to cooperate, using the conventions of film and television drama to secure the attention of the media and of us.

Early in the rush of power felt by the new Bush administration, an anonymous official took it on himself to boast of their ability to control perception. He told a reporter that they felt the "reality-based media" was obsolete: "When we act, we create our own reality." As Frank Rich commented in *The Greatest Story Ever Sold: The Decline and Fall of Truth from 9/11 to Katrina,* "The same conservatives who once deplored postmodernism and moral relativism were now eagerly promoting a brave new world in which it was a given that there could be no empirical reality in news, only the reality you wanted to hear (or that they wanted you to hear)."

At its most innocent, the effort consisted of what Daniel Boorstin first identified as the "pseudo-event," in which a ceremony was staged for a compliant press, and broadcast as if it were real. We've come a long way since then. Not that such events don't continue, but now everyone understands the device and is inclined to judge it on its theatrical merits. President George W. Bush's now-legendary carrier landing celebrating the "end" of the war in Iraq took the form to new levels. It was in certain ways the perfect pseudo-event, a contrived piece of stagecraft without any practical purpose, whose value was entirely symbolic.

But such events had better *be* perfect, because, for our part, we have all gotten terribly savvy about this sort of thing. Indeed even as the event is under way the observers in the media start talking not about the event itself but about the strategy behind it, and how effective it is likely to be, and we viewers expect them to provide such criticism. By doing so they restore their sense of self, suggesting that they are not hoodwinked, even though they are making the spectacle possible with their coverage. We enter right into this meta-reporting with enthusiasm, all of us shrewd critics of the president's "performance." And though one's feelings will be colored by politics, this analysis is really beyond partisanship. There is something a little degrading about the whole business, or so you might think—we are in effect judging our leaders on how successful they are in thinking of ways to deceive us. But so, in a way, like the reporters themselves, we rescue our dignity—by showing that we understand full well what's up and are coolly beyond outrage. There is little doubt that the air is filled with demagoguery, the half-lies, the full lies, the renaming and repackaging. We salvage self-regard only by maintaining that we ought to be able to keep a clear head on these subjects. No one is beating the bottoms of our feet with sticks. And we purchase this dignity at a cost, the cost of detachment.

Neal Gabler, in his characteristic extravagance, maintains that vast real-world events—wars, for instance—are organized for their dramatic content. And one suspects that he would claim that the whole Iraq war could be seen as motivated not by geopolitical or moral causes but by dramatic purposes. Indeed he says this explicitly about Gulf War I: "The Gulf War was formulated like a World War II picture. . . . It was meant to be short and sharp, its narrative lineaments clean, its heroes heroic and its mustachioed villain, Iraqi dictator Saddam Hussein . . . right out of the hoariest anti-Nazi propaganda." There is little reason to think that Gabler would feel any different about "Operation Iraqi Freedom," in which, he would no doubt argue, the theater became all the more brazen with the decision to allow a backstage view, through the real-time war reporting of "embedded" journalists.

It is appallingly true, at any rate, that we watched it as a spectacle. An exultant embedded journalist from CNN roared across the desert in a tank on the first day of the invasion, broadcasting live and shouting that this was "a first." But as the war dragged on, surely this sense of theatricality faded away. We knew we were witnessing not a stage tragedy but a real-life tragedy. At least we felt that we were more engaged, and perhaps we were. But you have to keep a cool eye on yourself when you are outraged over something that remains secondary to your life. From time to time the PBS evening news would show the photographs of soldiers killed in action ("here in silence are seven more"), and I would find myself standing there in the kitchen, looking up from the cutting board perhaps, or perhaps just holding a glass of wine from which I respectfully would not sip, and I would look at the screen and register the name and the age and the hometown, fleetingly imagining their lives, shaking my head sadly. And then I began to realize that there was something about this ritual that had nothing to do with pain on my part, something that was indeed shamefully self-enhancing.

A few weeks before his death I had lunch with an old friend and teacher, the literary and social critic Benjamin DeMott—the last time I would see him, as it turned out. He was writing something that would remain unfinished but was published many months later, on just this subject, the falsity of feeling that public tragedy can inspire, though it took a darker turn than I could allow myself. The essay was called "Battling the Hard Man" and it was a confessional about being addicted to violence—not violence enacted, of course, but violence observed from a mediated distance. "When, as happens, a newscast ends without casualty totals—for soldiers, or civilians, or both—impatience and aggravation follow. . . . I reach for the remote and commence surfing—grim look intact—for the missing numbers. . . . Wanting terrible news to be worse, relishing catastrophe whose bottom can't be sounded—this condition developed quite swiftly. . . . A key element in the condition, as comes clearer with time, is the accompanying cruelly neutral curiosity about what is happening to us inside and why—whether our occasional eruptions of 'moral concern' have any weight whatever."

The essay seemed to have passed by, exciting little or no attention. It may have been extravagant. But what I liked about it was not just its honesty, the honesty of a dying man, but its emphasis on consciousness as well. Although media are implicated, the blame is upon us. It is finally self-indulgent to blame the screen, any screen, for our failures of imagination. Our problem is not movies or television. It is whatever quality is within us that cannot connect with other lives. We can't blame technology for our mendacities, for that we cannot even blame our mendacious leaders. We have ourselves to blame for our renegade feelings. And if we can't control them, we ought at least to face them. We must, to borrow a fine discredited phrase, win back our own "hearts and minds."

4. Weeping Nation

I CRY MORE THESE DAYS. It seems as if I went for about three decades without tears, all the way from childhood to the beginning of middle age. This can't be completely true, and in fact I do recall one exception. I had been on the phone with my father and things had come to a pretty pass for him, and when the call ended I was utterly astonished to hear my own involuntary sob. That was that and it was memorable for its uniqueness, and for what I think of now as its honesty.

I cry more these days—and in this I seem to be a good citizen. A few years back the women invited the men to start crying; I think the women regretted it at once, but the damage was done. Most men turned out not to be very good at crying. Spontaneity, like every other damn thing, takes practice. But nonetheless the world began to smile on tears. And now our culture grows ever more weepy. Is it a good thing? We seem to think so.

Turn on the television. Memorial Day. A high school

band is marching. This would not be newsworthy except that the band members have each "adopted" a Second World War veteran in their hometown, and march in honor of the soldiers. One of the old guys is interviewed on camera. How does it feel? He is long practiced in modesty. We just did our duty, don't know what all the fuss is about, he says. But the interviewer presses: How does it feel that these young people have shown an appreciation for what you, the greatest generation, did for them? It is hard for the man to say it means a lot, and when he does the voice breaks. And that's a wrap. "I'm Somebody Somebody, Eyewitness News."

I sometimes think that there should be a warning about televised tears, like those goofy redundant advisories when the gory pictures are coming: "The following contains graphic images." *Warning: the following contains choked sobs, quivering chins, and some actual tears. Viewer discretion is advised.*

But tears have become part of the currency of meaning in public life. They are a convenient language of validation. He's crying: he must really be sincere.

Another veteran appears on the evening news, just a day or so later; this one was badly wounded in the current war. He has returned legless. His hometown, somewhere in the South, has rallied behind him. They are building him a house. Volunteer labor, donated materials. It won't cost him a penny. A guy being interviewed on the job keeps wielding his trowel, too busy to look up at the camera, mumbling something about just trying to help out. The legless man is shown playing in a sandbox with his daughter. He humbly expresses his gratitude to the townspeople. The voice-over says of the veteran, "He doesn't think about what he has lost." (Beat) "He thinks about what he has gained."

Appallingly, my eyes mist. *We are good people. We help our neighbors. We take care of our own. Much benefit comes out of suffering.* . . . And what a service the newscast has provided for me. The little moment has offered me a chance to forget about the war, to forget all the other maimed people and the dead, to forget even the essential fact of the life of the veteran himself, and others like him, who forty years hence, still will have no legs.

Again and again, on the television—in the newspapers too but especially on my beloved television—we are kindly given these opportunities to subvert with sentiment what we know to be the rule in the world. The billionaire has established the scholarship fund for his old grade school, the homeless fellow has returned the lost satchel full of cash, the soldier has patched the wounds of the enemy: wealth is not selfish, poverty not mean, war is not even hell. And day after day these little sentimental subversions welcome us to mindlessness.

If I were a teacher of the very young I would try to get them to understand big numbers, especially 300 million, the population of our country, and 6.5 billion, the population of the world. You would think that these numbers would have inclined us toward the big picture, but instead they have propelled us backward. We seem to have lost a taste for abstraction. We live in the age of the personalization of everything.

There in the balcony, with the First Lady, sits the fellow who is tonight's symbol. Is it a decorated hero of the controversial war, a victim of the disease the president intends to cure, a police officer who has taken a bullet defending our borders from the illegals? It doesn't much matter, because no one knows the symbol now and no one will remember him or her an hour from now, but for a blinding moment the symbol will rise and receive the standing ovation of the Congress and the cabinet and the warm gaze of the demurely applauding First Lady. In recent administrations we came to expect that the State of the Union address would include the person in the balcony, or a generous offering of stories about "ordinary Americans from all walks of life." All politics are local, said the venerated former Speaker of the House. It may still be true, but it is more precisely true today to say that all politics are personal, which is not at all the same thing. That is, our political life doesn't depend on a direct relationship between the governed and the governing, it depends on the ability of the governing to tell stories about the governed, to speak as if they know us. Franklin Roosevelt, who may well have started this with his fireside chats, would nonetheless be astonished to see where we are now. If he were to give his Four Freedoms speech today, it would have to involve someone with a name like *Anna-Mae who will go to bed hungry tonight unless we give her freedom from want.* Ideas in public discourse seem only to become real when they become embodied in some symbolic figure. This is sometimes nefarious—"Willie Horton" or the "Welfare Queen." But more often the symbol is a deserving figure, embattled, maybe, put-upon, sacrificing: the overtaxed small-business owner who thus endorses a tax cut for the rich, the brave firefighter who signifies the generosity of our government with its grants to departments like his, the teacher who insists on high performance from her students: the person in the balcony. And—this may be naïve—it doesn't seem to me to be all cool manipulation that drives our leaders at these moments. Ronald Reagan is said to have believed the whoppers he told, and in a way I think all presidents may believe such extravagances—to concentrate the vast power of your presidency on some anonymous person must feel a lot like love.

It is not only politicians who seek to "put a human face" on issues. Journalists have been doing so longer and they do it better, and now it is a convention we could scarcely imagine living without. But increasingly it has become more than a method, it has become a mode of understanding. What used to be known as a "human interest story" is now the news itself. Look at almost any front page of the *New York Times* catapulting some anonymous figure into symbolic truth. *Jane Smith spreads out the quarters and nickels and dimes on her kitchen table. Payday isn't until Friday. . . . When Bill White is asked where it all started, he thinks back to the pain he ignored in his shoulder. . . . Like all the girls in the neighborhood, Mary Jones felt she needed body art. . . .*

And what's wrong with this? Is not human understanding what we seek? Well, yes, it is. And didn't the poet say that the proper study of mankind is man? Right again. But as the parade of faces goes by, vivid then gone, vivid then gone, you begin to ask what we understand from these people. We don't understand them, surely—they are mere snapshots of themselves, and it would be arrogant of us to think that we know anything about them. More to the point, we seldom understand the issue they represent, which is inevitably more complicated than their involvement in it. The problem is that we think we know something that we don't know. We don't know, but we have the feeling of knowing. The personalization of everything invites the sentimentalization of everything.

As I say, I cry more these days. Not cleansing tears, though, just the misty sort. The welling up, the sometimes overbrimming. I mist at the touching stories in the news, at the odd commercial. And worst of all at my own generous thoughts. They are treacherous things, these tears. Because they are not about what they seem to be about. They are not expressions of feelings, but self-congratulation on the fact of having feelings. They celebrate feeling anything at all. Tears like this are to emotion as derivatives are to the stock market. We are drowning all of us in a sea of mawkishness.

May I speak for a moment about animals? We love our dogs, of course, and cats too, can talk about them for hours. He thinks he's human, we say. People smile. Their cat thinks so too. And now the Whole Foods company has reached out to the lobster, has decided not to sell live lobsters in its stores because the creatures suffer too much by being confined to tanks. Free the lobster. One wonders if anyone thought of the clam, littlenecks and quahogs so famously happy in their mudflats.

We name our laws after the victims of crimes. We like our Olympic stars best if they have survived a near-fatal plane crash or if their uncle, once a luge man himself, is on life support, just hanging on until they run the course. Hail to all the deserving who beat the odds, to the one-armed Little Leaguer, the orphan plucked from a desperate continent for open-heart surgery in bountiful Boston, the tottering bride and groom married at last after sixty years apart.

Meanwhile, the great ponderous intractable horrors roll on, and about these, we sigh. We deplore them. And we talk about them, and as we talk—the tragedy, the incompetence— we grow more animated. Little half-smiles play about the edges of our mouths.

It is common to lament the Disneyfication of the physical world, and I do it all the time, but I sometimes think our tacky commercial landscape is as nothing compared with the world of manufactured feeling that warms the heart like a microwave. Behind all this gauzy emotion play the shadows of things we don't want to think about: the mayhem done in our name, the people we have abandoned—all the indifference we feel to the fate of millions of our fellows, are compelled, really, to feel if we are going to get through our day with any efficiency. Chris Hedges remarks in his book *War Is a Force That Gives Us Meaning*, "Those in war swing from rank sentimentality to perversion, with little in between. Stray puppies, street kids . . . anything that can be an object of affection for soldiers are adopted and pampered even in the midst of killing." What is true in extremis has its counterpart in what we call ordinary life. Our moist-eyedness doesn't exist apart from our hardness of heart: they are of a piece. We have become, I fear, a culture of sentimentalists, and sentimentalists are dangerous people. I have no doubt that our current enemies, those who prefer to call us infidels, weep copious tears too.

5. Sincerity

JEDEDIAH PURDY GREW UP in what was called, in hippie days, "intentional poverty." His well-educated parents moved to a hill farm in West Virginia, where they cultivated the land with horses, grew much of their own food, and tried, in his father's words, "to pick out a small corner of the world and make it as sane as possible." The experiment worked, at least in the sense that the boy grew up with a unified vision of life, believed in the vision wholeheartedly, and continued to believe after he left for school (Exeter and Harvard). He said that his childhood gave him "perfect confidence in the reality of things."

Stepping into the larger world, Purdy encountered much he did not like. In 1999, when he was only twenty-four, he published a book called *For Common Things*, whose avowed aim was to speak out against what he considered a pervasive disease in the culture. Without much oversimplification, the disease could be identified by a single word: irony. Irony trivializes life. Irony prevents honest relationships. Irony forbids the declaration of values. Irony is a coward's evasion of feeling. So went his argument: "We practice a form of irony insistently doubtful of the qualities that would make us take another person seriously: the integrity of personality, sincere motivation, the ideal that opinions are more than symptoms of fear or desire."

He declared himself in favor of "straight talk." There can be few but the most cynical—that is, those most heavily armored against their own feelings—who have not felt a longing similar to the one that the young author describes. At the immediate level this is a very personal and universal desire, and yet it also has a particular purchase on our own society, one that has long valued straight talk.

But it would be hard to give up irony, wouldn't it? Irony, that charming roué—it would be a laughless world without him. Of course, I guess there's something circular about this idea: if you look at things one way, jokes are exactly the problem. Maybe a laughless world wouldn't be so bad if you could trade in the jollity for spiritual communion among beings. "Wit is the epitaph of an emotion," said the mighty Nietzsche. And the corollary of that is: If your emotions aren't dead, they don't need headstones.

Irony is more than laughs. Irony's real gift to discourse is its kindness in allowing you to say two things at once. And two-things-at-once is often enough exactly what you really mean. Sometimes you want to say how charming and maddening someone is, how angry and how forgiving you are, or how sorry and yet guiltless you feel.

And we are talking only about the petty irony of daily life. Irony is vital to art high and low, where irony becomes not an obscurer but an enlightener of thought and feeling. There is no confusion about the purity of Swift's sentiments in *A Modest Proposal*. The popular music that has always meant the most to me has been the music my parents listened to. Masters of irony were the old lyricists. "My Funny Valentine," half of whose words sound like rank insult. (Is your figure less than Greek?) Or "You're the Top," with that comic sort of hyperbole that makes you wonder.

Imagine a world without Swift or "My Funny Valentine"! Imagine a world without New York exaggeration or North Dakotan understatement or the drollery of Maine.

After the attacks of September 11, 2001, the editor of *Vanity Fair* magazine, of all people, proclaimed the "end of irony"—finally an event had come along that could be spoken of in only humble and direct and unaffected tones. Happily, the obituary was premature. The great tragedy was briefly thought to be the force, à la the Second World War, that would unite a culture as never before. But inevitably—mercifully—the reality set in, a jumble of idealism and self-interest. The "events of September eleventh" found their way into fiction, and in perhaps the best of the new novels,

Claire Messud's *The Emperor's Children,* the author gave us a delicious portrait of hypocritical grief in Murray Thwaite, the novel's monstrous antihero, a literary lion and "public intellectual" of surpassing self-regard. His nephew is missing and presumed dead. As it happens he loathes the boy. On a television panel he is asked about the tragedy and he "bowed his silver head—a gesture that could be construed as respect, or resignation, or dismay at the interviewer's crass intrusion—and said, 'Some things are family matters. It's an indescribable loss. And ours is just one of thousands.'"

For a thousand such reasons, let's not get rid of irony.

But we do want a set of public manners that allows for directness. I want, at least sometimes, something from myself and others—from ordinary conversation and from the general discourse that sets the tone of our public life—something like the quality of directness that Jedediah Purdy celebrates. There's a word for it, "sincerity," but it's such a poor, battered, discredited term that everyone hesitates to use it. "Sincere" may often enough serve as faint praise for the hapless. ("At least he's sincere.") And we suspect people who even marginally overdisplay the mannerisms of sincerity—the earnest gaze, the firm handshake, the careful attention to one's name ("Tell me, Bob . . .")—of only imitating sincerity and thus perpetrating social fraud. Books have been written to tell people how to seem sincere, most notably the bestseller of decades ago, *How to Win Friends and*

Influence People. Sincerity is one of those concepts that doesn't make much sense without its implied opposite, and indeed "insincere" is the far more vigorous word.

Suppose you set out to be sincere. What would you do? Well, stop lying—that would be a start, surely.

Not that it's so easy. Several years ago Sissela Bok wrote a well-received book called *Lying,* in which, of course, she deplored the practice as corrosive to society. But the most interesting part of the book was its little codicils providing release from the burdens of truth-telling in one situation or another (e.g., "Lying to Liars"). We have all told social lies, overpraised or falsely forgiven, and we have all been the recipients of them. To tell such "white lies" often makes me feel virtuous but also covertly superior. To receive them sometimes stirs resentment, but sometimes not, depending on the circumstances. (Depending, for instance, on whether you think the dissembler "sincerely" feels warm toward you, even if she doesn't think you look as dashing as she says.) But we all could swear off grand deceptions and these little politenesses and still not achieve sincerity.

Sincerity seems to want something more from us, something that makes it more like a gift. Sometimes, alas, it can be that most unpleasant of gifts—the obligatory one. It is characteristic of contemporary conversation that we tend to place a value on self-revelation. We haven't had a satisfying conversation unless we've gotten "something personal."

And to feel under pressure to deliver some little revelation is to feel that particular kind of discomfort that can't be voiced.

Sincerity is often described in metaphors of transparency, and indeed "open" serves as a contemporary word of high praise. "Open" means having nothing to hide, and more: a willingness to share one's interior life. I am not sure about this metaphor myself. Do I want to be an open book? A glass box? Do I want you to be one? I might prefer solidity, a block of wood, which when cut reveals itself to be without veneer, the same inside and out, if perhaps a darker color at the core. Or an onion, with many layers, but all onion. It is all I can ask of myself or others—really, all I want—but even that is a lot.

It is interesting to think that this quality that seems central to our lives has not always been so, that sincerity, like interstate commerce or ballroom dancing, has a history. In *Sincerity and Authenticity* (1971), Lionel Trilling points out that the word shows up in the early sixteenth century, meaning simply whole or pure, and then is quickly transformed into a metaphorical usage similar to its meaning today. It was a time, Trilling points out, of rapid social change in Europe, of the sudden emergence of a middle class, of social mobility, a time when people had reason to doubt one another as they had not before.

Our interest in sincerity has occurred in waves—like

much cultural history it's both cyclical and cumulative, like a wheel turning, showing different sides of itself, but always rolling in one direction. The direction has been always toward enlargement of one's obligations to be a sincere person.

The English philosopher Bernard Williams (in *Truth and Truthfulness*) comes at the question in a different way: he suggests that sincerity is not so much a willed activity as an instinctual act. In that sense, it represents a kind of character trait, more a matter of heart than mind: "Sincerity basically involves a certain kind of spontaneity, a disposition to come out with what one believes, which may be encouraged or discouraged, cultivated or depressed, but is not itself expressed in deliberation and choice."

This is a tantalizing idea. It is true that life has few gifts (to give or to receive) more gratifying than unfeigned laughter or surprise. It is a sad fact, maybe, but true, that most lovers would rather inspire the involuntary cry of pleasure than a carefully composed sonnet. And so too a candid, "unguarded" opinion from a public figure may seem worth more than a considered speech.

But what is to be treasured as an occasional gift may be feared as a standard. To insist on perfect spontaneity may lead only into a vortex of doubt and suspicion. To put it another way, orgasms are easier to fake than poems. Once "spontaneity" is valued, some people will become very good at appearing spontaneous.

It has already happened. In the mid-nineteenth century, American society created what the historian Karen Halttunen calls a "cult of sincerity," a code of behavior (manners, fashion, moral precepts) that cherished emotional trustworthiness, and shunned hypocrisy. Spontaneity was a high virtue. Halttunen suggests (in her book *Confidence Men and Painted Women*) that this "cult" came in reaction to the upheaval in the young country that happened around 1830 (the same upheaval that altered architecture and furniture) the sudden mercantilization of a previously agrarian society. Everything was fluid, social roles were up for grabs. Most important, people, unmoored from fixed roles in stable communities, often proved not to be what they seemed to be. A wealth of advice literature appeared counseling youth on how to avoid the perils of deception in urban life, where the representative villain was the "confidence man," who used the pretense of earnest concern to fleece his victims.

Halttunen documents what became little less than a cultural obsession with the menace of hypocrisy and deceit. At a certain moment, she recounts, the struggle moved indoors: that is, it was widely felt that true sincerity was impossible in the world of commerce or politics. The parlor was the proper place to play the game, and the referees became women. Women were thought to be naturally superior in sensibility anyway, and it was the spontaneous demonstration of feeling that proved them so: "a flow of feeling that cannot be restrained," as one contemporary writer put it.

The changes in the trappings of the social world were extraordinary. Women's clothes, though they may seem elaborate enough to modern eyes, over the course of just a few years had undergone a vast transformation, the heavily ornamented costumes of the early part of the century yielding to dresses with simple lines meant to convey lack of pretense, openness of heart. Feathered chapeaux gave way to modest cloth bonnets. The costumes may look hopelessly frilly now, but in context they made a statement equivalent to designer jeans and T-shirts.

At the same time, old rules of etiquette, with their emphasis on scrupulous self-restraint, came under suspicion: proper behavior was meant to be spontaneous and natural— "right feelings from a right heart," in a phrase of the time. But manners and fashion have always been about separating sheep from goats, so it was necessary that strict rules of behavior remain, and all the more so in a society in flux, with many people seeking certification. No less self-restraint was necessary in the new world of sincerity, but it had to pretend not to *be* restraint. Halttunen describes the rituals of entertaining, which she calls "the genteel performance"; its stage was the parlor. Before one could get to the parlor and be greeted by one's hostess, it was customary to go directly (with the help of a servant) to a sort of offstage area, with dressing rooms for each sex devoted to arranging hair and costume. Any irregularity in appearance, any sign of the difficulties of arrival (a flushed face, for instance) would be a breach, but worse would be the public effort to repair it. Thus one was expected to arrive at the parlor in a state of perfect composure, and to be received by a hostess equally tranquil and seemingly without concerns.

As with gesture, so too with language. The rule governing spoken discourse was tact, which in large measure consisted of not letting down one's guard, not acknowledging the strenuous effort required to appear effortless. If a servant dropped a plate, it went unmentioned.

The historian has some sport with the hypocrisy of affected naturalness, but, I don't know, it sounds not wholly unpleasant to me. More to the point, it's not as if we view this scene from some new world of social liberation. In a sense, a century of manners, ever more frank, casual, "open," and informal, has been only a refinement—or a coarsening, depending on how you look at it—of the same sincere ideal: seeming to be unfettered by pretense, all the while watching oneself and others for subtle signifiers of station. (In our own time the game has taken on the additional hypocrisy of faux egalitarianism, the cult of the regular guy.)

But they were obsessed, the Victorians, and it's instructive to see the particular way in which they tied themselves in knots. Letters are a particularly rich indicator of their ideals. Avowals of sincerity were standard fare, and so were recitations of the importance of sincerity; indeed the word was touched and retouched like an amulet. A young woman praises her suitor: "His behavior here was polite without affectation, and an air of sincerity appeared in all he said." As Halttunen writes, "Young lovers protested their sincerity at every turn and often devoted the substance of their discussion to the abstract importance of sincerity in matters of love."

So antique, so bizarre. We are beyond all that, we are irreverent and self-mocking, we speak in air quotes and we sign it xoxo. And yet what energy goes, still, into the simple assertion "I mean it."

It is worth remembering what led to the "cult of sincerity"—it was a distrust in public life. Corruption, deceit, falsity: these were the things of the street, of the public forum. Only at home could an honest society flourish. This is a gift of very dubious worth from the nineteenth century. It continues to pervert our expectations of public life.

Doubting that ceremony or oratory can be "sincere," we insist that our public personalities—especially our politicians—demonstrate their private side. No matter that the contradiction is irresolvable: once it's public it's no longer private. Thus we are treated to newsmagazine specials on the candidate at home—intimate, grainy black-and-white photos (by convention, if counterintuitively, black-and-white is more "real" than color) of the candidate "alone" with his wife, the candidate "cutting brush" on his ranch.

And cutting brush is a lot better than, say, windsurfing when it comes to the realness quotient of the politician. Real people are supposed to do things that ally themselves with other real people. It is odd that we demand that our candidate doesn't think he's better than anybody else (even though he's running for an office that requires him to lead a nation of 300 million people, command the most powerful army in the world, make decisions that affect virtually all other peoples of the earth, requires him in a word to be better, a lot better). We want the guy to be sincere, we want him to be just like everybody else.

Our poor leaders. It is not burden enough for them to sentimentalize us; they must also sentimentalize themselves. "Who would you rather have a beer with?" became a semiserious question in evaluating candidates, and the answer quite a good predictor of victory. We have always had a strain in our politics (and on the whole a healthy strain) that mocked pomp and rewarded plainness. We have long celebrated modest origins—Lincoln the "rail-splitter" the classic example. Daniel Webster once lamented that he had not been born in a log cabin. He in fact began life in fairly pinched circumstances, a New Hampshire hill farm, but when he rose to heights of wealth and influence as a lawyer and statesman no one expected him to pretend still to be a yeoman, cutting brush on the weekend. Things have changed. Now we have people of exalted origins who pretend to have matured into "regular guys."

Say what one will about Richard Nixon (and one will), but he seems to be the last elected American president who did not have to pretend to be a regular guy. (Perhaps in part because Nixon all too demonstrably was, in an unhappy sense, a regular guy—he radiated one of the less agreeable aspects of ordinariness, social anxiety.) The first President Bush, certifiably upper class, was so bad at pretending to be a regular guy—amazed at the supermarket scanner—that he could be forgiven his efforts. But his son took the charade to the level of theatrical art, his unabashed invocations of God, his big cowboy belt buckle, his dropped *g's*, his *idn'ts* and *dudn'ts*. Aficionados of this technique would listen for the little signs that authenticated it as a performance—the Andover *rahther* that would pop up from time to time, the way the accent would shift with the degrees of longitude as he made his way west into the "heartland." It was splendid.

Less good was the attempt of his rival in the 2004 election, the hapless Kerry. Yes, he rode a motorcycle onstage on the Leno show. Yes, he lined up with his wartime buddies. Yes, he wore fashions by the working-class couturier Carhartt. But he was up against it. For one thing, he could not persuade his vastly wealthy, foreign-born wife to speak with the chumminess of a truckstop waitress. He dropped a few *g's* himself, but could not bring himself to lose an accent learned on Naushon Island and at St. Paul's School. He was, probably on those grounds alone, toast.

Many found it astounding in that election that so many people could vote contrary to their economic interests, but

in fairness the winning side had more than a superior sentimental hero, it had a superior sentimental message as well.
What is money compared with myth, and the myths that
were offered to the public were powerful. They were myths
such as American exceptionalism, the power of the individual, and faith in God. However these myths do or don't accord with the truth, they have one other highly attractive
quality: to voice them allowed people to feel not only better
about themselves but better than many of their fellows. I
am the patriot, I am strong and self-reliant, and God is on
my side.

When the 2008 election hove into view, the appetite for an
authentic candidate had only sharpened. Indeed, more than
one pundit called it "the year of authenticity." What was
meant? Various things, to be sure: consistency and integrity,
even simple likability, but always more than that—a sense
that the person was whole and that we were getting the
whole person, that nothing was left in the greenroom.
Sometimes this hunger took a strange form: the affable
Southern governor scored unexpected primary victories on
the strength of his unpretentious good humor, and no matter that he thought the earth was created in seven days or that
the vision of him in the White House evoked musical comedy. He was authentically benighted. Senator McCain had

more serious claims on the imagination, an "authenticity" derived of his suffering as a prisoner of war in North Vietnam, and a reputation for candor, which was, to be sure, somewhat compromised when he had, during his previous campaign, turned it into a brand name by calling his bus the "Straight Talk Express." Despite his own "flip-flopping" on issues, his years of unprotected dialogue with the press continued to help him. One columnist, Nicholas Kristof in the *New York Times*, praised McCain backhandedly for his ineptitude in "pandering" to his audience, remarking that "when he does try double-talk, he looks so guilty and uncomfortable that he convinces nobody."

In the case of Senator Clinton it was tempting to think she was in some way relieved of the obligation to prove her authenticity. She had perhaps been annealed by the scandals of her husband's behavior and the humiliation she bore because of them. It was as if the understory of her private life had been burned away by the fire of public scrutiny. Books appeared about her, and reviewers said, "Nothing new here." Maybe we did not want to know anything more. We felt that her "real life" had become her public life. I suppose this was all a dreamy, wistful thought. The senator seemed by general consensus to have revived her faltering campaign in New Hampshire by "a show of emotion"—a brief catch of the voice, a dampening of the eye. (Her foes criticized her for this vulnerability—some even thought it contrived—

even though it was nothing compared with the public weeping we routinely admire in 6'4" linebackers retiring from the game.)

But it was Barack Obama who was offering us his very *self.*

In 2004, it had seemed that the Democrats, to counter the Republican message of sentimental God-fearing jingo-ism, had only doubt and bad news, and the implicit message that "you need help." (What? We're Americans, we don't need help!) But the young Obama floated an alternative strategy before the party convention in his keynote speech, so eloquent a speech that it didn't sound like a strategy. He spoke of the unity of the American people, of the transcen-dence of national character over class and race and partisan divisions. It may be that our politics cannot escape senti-mentality of one kind or another. The vision the speech of-fered was indeed sentimental, and I, and millions, became sentimental over it. It congratulated us for something we have not achieved. Moreover it seemed to wish away true structural divisions in the society that pitted real interests against real interests. But it evoked a longing, and not an ignoble one. Forced to choose among sentimentalisms, I would pick that one.

The party failed to heed him in 2004, but Obama's speech didn't die with the election. It propelled his career forward, until four years later he was in pursuit of the prize himself. The strategy that Obama offered to his party, to seek (or to declare) commonality, now became his message, and the message became embodied in him. He was quite aware that he was offering authenticity: he referred to it in his campaign memoir *The Audacity of Hope*, as that quality "we long for . . . of being who you say you are, of possessing a truthfulness that goes beyond words." In him much of the truthfulness was in his skin color and his racially mixed blood: he was saying, I can transcend, thus can we. Slogans that might have seemed parodic in their vagueness— "hope," "change"—became charged with meaning.

People used the word "messianic" about him, and not without reason: For his black voters he might have represented mere triumph; for his white voters he seemed to offer something infinitely more valuable, absolution for centuries of sin. (Senator Clinton, who represented a rebuke to the only prejudice more universal than racism, misogyny, seemed to have no such effect.) The self-critical citizen had to ask: Do we love him, or do we love ourselves for embracing him so? The crowds chanted, "Yes we can!" But could we? Had we the will to go beyond desire? And the citizen of ordinary human sympathy had to ask: What about *him*? Can this man (could any man) endure such love?

We ask so much of our would-be leaders, more than they can conceivably give, and yet less in some sense than we should ask. We want their souls when we might better seek their minds. Some thirty years ago—before things had reached their current state—Richard Sennett wrote about the problem in *The Fall of Public Man*. He was arguing that what we call community is based on a forced and false intimacy, on bringing private relations into the public sphere. According to Sennett, we were losing "the essence of urbanity, which is that men can, together, act without the compulsion to be the same." We need a different set of rules. Not a hunger for personal understanding, but the true respect for difference that refuses to be understood, or to understand anyone else, too quickly. But the contrary impulse runs so deep in modern life that it is hard to imagine the world without it.

When his foes in government wanted to attack the man who was arguably the most commanding public figure of the last fifty years, Martin Luther King Jr., they sought to put together a dossier on his private sexual habits. We impeached a president for his similar misdeeds.

Inversions of public and private life take ever stranger turns. A member of Congress is portrayed with sympathy in the *New York Times* because she privately disdains what she did in a recent election—a political campaign of attack ads and misleading letters that "went out under her name." She speaks of these with "a look of disgust" on her face. "I was appalled by what I had to do," she says. The writer David Brooks then praises her for fighting "to preserve her own humanity." The private person is felt to be the "real" person. This predisposition is so ingrained that I feel a moment of sympathy for the woman. But this is very curious. On reflection, I think I would prefer that she had kicked her cat and carried on illicitly with her campaign manager, but "preserved her humanity" by not participating in a vicious campaign—that is, by behaving well in public.

Increasingly we lack forms and conventions of public life that have their own weight and consequence. I have seen these vanish in my own lifetime, like the fedoras that disappeared from men's heads after the election of John F. Kennedy. It is true that public dignity covered a multitude of private sins, but there is no indication that the sins have grown any fewer. Hypocrisy wears a fresher, more "natural" face, and it falls harder when it falls. We can be vicious in our delight in hypocrisy revealed. The senator—outspoken foe of same-sex marriage, defender of "family values"—gets arrested for attempting to solicit sex in an airport men's room. We pounce on his "hypocrisy."

I too felt an unseemly delight. But then you think. It's the public policies you should be against, not the private behavior. A compassionate public, a public less confused about the very nature of privacy, would suddenly feel not contempt but compassion for this poor devil. Indeed if you opposed his policies, is he not exactly the sort of victim of sexual oppression, forced into covert behavior, that you want to shelter from a hostile society?

Hypocrisy! Of all the things to be worried about. Great wisdom, not cynicism, inheres in the maxim: "Hypocrisy is the homage that vice pays to virtue." We need more people, standing for something worthy, something beyond themselves, something they perhaps unavoidably fail to achieve in their private lives. Let us forgive them their little sins and hold them to account for their great ones. I think we might try to judge them by what they believe and what they do in the world at large, not by what they "are." I think it might be better not to destroy but to enhance the distinction between public and private life, even at the price of hypocrisy.

PART IV

The Unicorn in the Looking Glass

1. Reflection

IN THE DIM UPSTAIRS ROOM of the Cluny Museum, in Paris, hangs the mysterious set of six tapestries known together as *La Dame à la Licorne*. I have seen them just twice and both times have stood before them transfixed, and I can't imagine how familiar with them one would have to be before the wonder ceased.

Their sheer size, and the astonishing richness of the color and detail, and the uncanny depth: you can gaze at the tapestries for some time seeing not much more than that. And the strangeness of the scenes depicted: the tall Lady, her maidservant, the stylized bestiary of real and imaginary animals—dog, monkey, lion, unicorn. The intricacy of the stitches: too much for anyone to do in a lifetime, and yet the whole so suffused with a single sensibility that it is hard to imagine it as anything but a work of individual genius. When I first understood that the tapestries illustrate the five senses, the very mundanity of this fact seemed only to intensify the otherworldliness of the work. How could such a simple concept inspire such consummate artistry? The sixth tapestry makes one realize that something more mysterious is afoot; the Lady stands under a banner reading *"A Mon Seul Désir,"* and the meaning of the image inspires perennial debate. Is she renouncing the senses, or is she celebrating that sense that lies beyond taste and touch and the rest, the sense experienced only by the heart? And the question propels one backward into the other scenes and complicates them too.

Although the tapestries are the work of a world governed by moral and spiritual rules virtually incomprehensible to us, they seem also to collapse time. Standing before them the second time, I found myself struck not by the distance but by the strange nearness of the fifteenth century. Once anyone did anything this complex, the creation of the computer, for example, looked like a foregone conclusion. Can the circuitry of a microchip be more complex? And in a completely different way there lurks in the fabric a pervasive wit that would seem to prefigure every modernist notion about the mystery of the self. It cannot be an accident that at the center of the center tapestry, "Sight," is the image that draws one in with such paradox and delight: the Unicorn stares into a looking glass held for him by the Lady.

When an imaginary beast sees his own reflection, what is it that he sees?

2. Not Ideas about the Thing . . .

THE RIPPLED GLASS of the windowpanes. Spring rain. A wall of green outside: trees in the mist. The stone fence. I look out the window, I look down at my hand, its one crippled finger. Stone, water, leaf, flesh. The checkbook on the desk—though in a sense more real than rain, considering its power to constrain my life—seems something of an abstraction, leading as it does to the great world of obligation and choice. Sometimes the mind wants only what the eye can see, the here-ness of the tangible, a table, a tool, and sometimes words that have passed beyond words.

In Wallace Stevens's poem "Not Ideas about the Thing but the Thing Itself," the poet, coming out of sleep on a morning in earliest spring, hearing a birdsong outside the window, thinks at first that he is in the hallucination of dreams, but then awakens to the fact of sun and the faint song. "That scrawny cry—it was /A chorister whose c preceded the choir. . . . It was like / a new knowledge of reality."

It is not, I think, a poem of resurrection or rebirth or of anything at once so grand, familiar, and thematic—it is, to my ear anyway, a poem about the simple solace we find in the immediacy of the world. We turn to the physical world for many things but often for the reassurance of our own reality.

The oldest Windsor chair, in the corner, is damaged, a crack in its arm. Somebody sat down too hard. It is embarrassing to admit how much this saddens me. The thing has endured two hundred years and now it has broken under my brief care. It seems to one part of my mind irrational, even vaguely blasphemous to animate an object so, but its wound feels like a crack in me. As with the chair, so with the landscape. I care (overmuch, no doubt) about the field up the road and hope this landscape, like so many others, stays intact. I hate the excesses and gross imprecision of public life, but I hate even more the falsity of feeling they evoke from me. So it is, I suppose, with the various subjects I have touched on in these pages. We seek a real world to find a real self.

Lately I have begun to memorize poems. It didn't start with poems, actually. It started with a road trip.

She: "We should know our presidents."

I: "Of course we should."

She: "I have a book."

This seemed, to be candid, a very bizarre idea. But then I thought of a perfectly sound reason for it. Sooner or later some examining physician, checking on whether you are headed down one of those dim unwelcoming corridors, will ask you to name the last four or five presidents in reverse order. How nice, I thought, to be able to roll on backwards down the list through Taft, Roosevelt, McKinley, Cleveland, Harrison and then to ask the man in the white coat if he would like to continue. So I fell to my task. And by Stonington we knew them. Very satisfying.

It was then I started to learn the great sonnets. I have never had much use for people who spout long stretches of *Paradise Lost* that they memorized in school. I don't recite aloud, but I say the poems nonetheless, to myself, in the dark. *For thy sweet love remembered such wealth brings.* Why do this? I have wondered, and I think it is essentially the same impulse that makes some men tinker with machines. It is the simple pleasure of knowing something in all its finite comprehensible parts. The nuts and bolts and washers of art.

3. Memory

THERE IS MEMORIZATION, and then there is memory, that un-willed and most chimerical thing. We need scarcely be re-minded of the unreliability of memory, of course, the mind's little tricks, and big ones too. Freud alerted us to "screen memories," and a dubious trade in "recovered memories" opened up a few years ago among certain psychother-apists. For literary and cinematic art the vagaries of memory have been a source of peculiar fascination (and in my view rather a one-trick pony). But for all that, are there not memories that we cannot and simply will not doubt? Bright, hard-edged fragments in the mind, shards of a broken pot that can never be reassembled—what would you have, who would you be, without them?

I hear a light plane overhead and—how often has this happened?—I am transported to a moment in childhood, alone, lying on the grass near the big rock on a summer af-ternoon, hearing just that sad, lazy drone. The sound stirs such a persistent melancholy that it must have done so then: this must be sadness remembered. People speak of "the wonder of childhood," but they mean more nearly the opposite of wonder—the blissful acceptance of the immediate and the blissful ignorance of all else. But one day something happens, a plane flies overhead, and it is like strangers' voices in another room, or a face glimpsed in a passing train, a sudden apprehension of the mystery and indifference of the world, one's aloneness in it.

The war years, my earliest memories, are bathed in sunlight. Tens of millions of people are being killed somewhere. But of the war I know only the cutout figures of the Grumman Hellcats on my blanket chest. Who has put them there? Doubtless my father, off now on a naval ship, known by his voice on a recording he had somehow sent home. Winter sunlight streams in on the pictures on the blanket chest, and dust motes dance in the light. Now I am outside, "bundled up," squinting against the cold sun on the blinding snow, on my way to the turkeys my grandfather is raising. Now I am plucking the pin feathers from a slaughtered bird. So few the images of the little farm, and yet it seems I have been trying to get back there all my life.

In the fifties it always seemed to be dark or rainy. A father home was less wonderful than a father away on a heroic mission. My parents, I later understood, had more money but greater desires too, and thus they were poorer than when they were merely penniless.

In some way all of us schoolchildren were aware of the world's menace. But what was it? The bomb? Everyone of a certain age likes to recall hiding under a school desk to take shelter against fallout. But was any child really frightened of a nuclear bomb? Not me, not anyone I knew. We were frightened of—uneasy about—something, though. There is perhaps a moment of group-memory, more telling than the A-bomb drills. It is the moment of discovery—in *Life* magazine?—of the stacked corpses of the victims, the emaciated bodies of survivors, of the concentration camps. It was nothing one would talk of to an adult. And adults would never talk about it to you. It was seen alone or with a friend, covertly. The adults had much on their mind and we knew that many things were off-limits, out-of-bounds for them. The world shrank. We were asked not to think about a lot, about all the things they did not want to think about. There was much to be done, and it all had to do with refinement, with rising in the world. Objects not seen before became necessary objects. Chafing dishes and cigarette boxes. Cocktail napkins with witty sayings in "Fractured French." Grand and awful events had happened, yes, and very recently, but that was over now. One night a week I would watch *Victory at Sea* on television. The stirring music. Richard Rodgers. (Later the song would have words: "No other love have I . . .") The destroyer rising from the rolling gray waves, plunging again, taking water over the bow. My father had been on the vast ocean, but now he was selling coated cloth with a made-up name: Fabricoid. Nothing glorious would ever happen again; history was over.

How few memories remain from our first seven or eight, or even ten or twelve years of life. Fragments without connections: my father at his basement desk dictating sales reports to the home office, making little green disks on the Soundscriber, sending them off in the mail. "Period. Paragraph. That's all." A particularly rainy day outside my classroom window with greens of the trees electrically vivid. A time of germ phobia, at the racetrack with my father, not wanting to touch doorknobs. The red face of a panicked classmate—I am in a heartless pack of boys on bicycles, chasing him. The smell of inner tubes at the beach. Clipping the hedge, the muscular arms of my father, bigger than other men's: he has worked for a living.

As I summon up these memories, only one animates itself into more than an image, and interestingly it is about not telling the truth. It was nighttime in our suburban home. I was in bed but not sleeping. I could hear my parents' voices. Talking about me. "Well, he's an honest boy," says my father. The implication is that my mother is not so sure. And she has it right. At eight or nine years old, I was a thief. I had shoplifted, have been caught, confessed. In the next frame, with my father, I return the stolen goods to the Firestone Store, and then in the car returning home, just as we bump across a railroad crossing, my father emits a single sob. It is the only time in my life I will hear the sound. I can never now tell him the full truth: that even in confessing I have lied. They do not know how much I took. One morning soon I will creep from the house before dawn to throw away the rest of the loot—including, oddly, a padlock, the only item I now recall—into the swamp. The crime haunted me for years. It was as if my very nature had been defined and condemned. But then, of course, it faded, became a sadness, then an anecdote.

Could I, with time and concentration, enumerate every remembered moment from these years? Maybe so, and even in their multitude they would be a tabletop jigsaw puzzle begun by an ambitious child on a rainy day and abandoned forever when the sun came out. More to the point. It would be a jigsaw puzzle with multiple solutions, because these memories were made when the mystery of family experience could not even be conceived. If memory is the very DNA of self-conception, then it is also the source of the unanswerable riddle, how to make these clues cohere.

It is said that pain fades and pleasure remains. Time softens memories, but there seems no moment in my past so remote that the fresh sting of remembered embarrassment or shame cannot bring a color to my cheek. From nowhere they come, and I wince or even mutter aloud to drive away these memories, some of them from forty or more years back. Kind letters not answered. Thoughtless insults rendered. I have had more than my share of joy—but how abstract it is in memory! Joy's moments do not come rushing back. It doesn't surprise you with its presence and you cannot recapture it at its height. It is more distant, disembodied, like a painting of oneself at an earlier, comelier time.

Yet, strangely, so in a way are the ineradicable sins distant, held at bay. Let one stand for many. I failed to rescue my dying father from a house plunged into madness and despair by his illness. But I cannot hold this time in my memory whole. I see it in flashes, see myself now in a strange, oblique memory: I remember going to the beach near my parents' retirement house, flailing about in the not-very-fearsome surf. I had just told my mother that she could not care for my father any longer, that he should go to a nursing home. Both tact and force deserted me. I did it clumsily. She told him what I had said, and they closed ranks and both rebuffed me. Nearly forty, I felt like a child again. I set out to swim and the strength left my body. I didn't have the courage even to break through the waves and swim to deeper water. It is this way, I think, when true sins are recalled—they are too big to encompass. Mine produce now no sharp agony, only an inescapable weight. These are the things that are always with us—we are like a ship under full sail but dragging its anchor unseen across the sea floor. The great failures and misdeeds "lie too deep for tears."

If you have troubled to read even this handful of sentences—dispositive of nothing, not a time, a family, or of me—you would nonetheless be annoyed to hear that I had made the memories up. I didn't, of course. I didn't, though people do, as we see from time to time. If I were going to in-vent a past to account for myself it might be darker or more romantic: I might create a mother as volatile as mine was said to be in her youth, though my clearest early memory of her is of walking home from town in companionable silence on a night when it began to snow. (The memory was so vivid that I mentioned it to her years later. Of course she didn't recall it at all. Probably she was tired and her feet were cold and she was resentful that we didn't have enough money for a second car.) Or I would imagine a bereft but colorful childhood. I have since seen so many places that might provide a background more suitable to the spirit than any of my actual homes. I might borrow a childhood from a woman I briefly knew who told of living in various wild out-posts with her artist father. Perhaps I would be a year-round boy on the summer resort island of Cuttyhunk, my father a lobsterman howling in the winter on the bluff like Heathcliff with the rages that I only imagined were in him. I might grant myself a fascination and later a romance with a girl who in summer arrived by yacht, a white shirt over her swimsuit. Or perhaps it would be a windswept village in the Hebrides where I could take solitary comfort, after my walk from the far-off school, in the glow of a turf fire in the grate.

One does not have to venture far into autobiography to discover the perils—the horrors!—of the form. But in the last couple of decades of the twentieth century in America, memoir became an ascendant literary genre. It was not that the novel was "dead" or even that fiction had necessarily lost its vigor, but for some reason more authors who once might have written autobiographical fiction sought to remove the mask and present themselves as they were, or imagined themselves to be. This could seem a very honest thing to do, and a satisfying one to readers, because so many novels are in fact autobiographical, and whether they are or not, so many readers want to read them that way. The path was broken in a way by poetry, which earlier, with poets as diverse as the Beats and Robert Lowell and Sylvia Plath, came to revel in the confessional mode.

As readers we seem to have developed a rather avaricious hunger for revelation and particularly for other people's woes. Perhaps the memoir, with its pressures toward a seemly modesty, worked against a heroic sense. Then again, a peculiar vanity lurks in private sins turned into public revelation. For whatever reason, it became a commonplace observation that the characteristic literary memoir told a story of trial or self-destruction. Benjamin Kunkel (a young novelist, not, or not yet, a memoirist) complained in the *New York Times Book Review* that for the modern memoirist "Life is what happens to you, not what you do. Victim and hero are one."

There was thus a strange temptation facing the memoirist, and that was the temptation to make things a little worse than they were, or even a lot worse. In 2006, an improbable scandal erupted over the memoir *A Million Little*

Pieces, by James Frey, which described the author's down-and-out life as a drug addict. Or purported to describe that life—as it turned out, Frey had taken liberties with the facts, to make things more sordid than they actually were. In the book's most memorable hyperbole, a passage that described his three months in jail turned out to be based on an incarceration that lasted more like three hours. (The scandal was improbable not because of the author's misdeed but because of the extent of outrage over it—no serious critic had suggested that the book was a particularly good one, true or false.)

Then, a couple of years later, fresh scandal occurred around the publication of a "memoir" that was invented out of whole cloth. In *Love and Consequences,* Margaret B. Jones wrote a compelling account of her childhood as a part Native American foster child living among the street gangs of Los Angeles. But the author's name was actually Margaret Seltzer, she was Caucasian, and she grew up in prosperous Sherman Oaks, where she had a conventional family life and attended an Episcopal day school. No one was inclined to give her credit for imagination.

We want the truth, and intolerance for invention of any kind seems to grow. Mary Karr's memoir *The Liar's Club,* published in 1995, became a much praised model for the contemporary genre. It is interesting to wonder how it might have fared just a handful of years later. It described the

abuse the author suffered as a child, and her difficulty in un-
covering it, and the book made much of the workings of
memory. At the same time, it self-evidently created visual
detail and dialogue (a long and vastly entertaining account of
adult conversation as heard by a child) in a way that bothers
some purists today. I don't know why we have grown more
critical on this point. It may be simple familiarity, a matter of
the proliferation of fanciful or blatantly false memoirs,
which has made us feel as readers that we may be attending
a masked ball.

I have a certain odd sympathy for those memoirists who
make it up. I can well understand them, arranging their fingers against the light to cast menacing shadow figures on
the wall. It is the desire to find some way to render those
emotions that seem out of proportion to the events to
which they are actually attached in memory.

Once I failed to get into a boat. There was every good reason not to get in, in fact. It was a little sailboat and I didn't
really know how to sail yet; I was about fifteen years old.
Moreover, it was winter. In the little harbor, people were
racing dinghies in what was, probably still is, called "frostbit-
ing." I was urged to try it, and something stopped me. I
would not have drowned—a chase boat hovered nearby—
and I was not afraid of the pain, just the humiliation. I can
still see the boat nudging itself against the dock in the light
cold breeze. This is not the stuff of memoir. It is the stuff of

lunacy. Yet I wish I had sailed the boat . . . to have tried. Decades later the moment emerges in my imagination with fresh regret. I have the preposterous feeling that my life might have been different had I gotten into that boat. In the New York office where I worked a couple of summers later there was a woman of perhaps twenty-four or twenty-five, and the night she asked me to go home with her I would have gone, and this at last would be a worthy story. (I can imagine it, and it would be thrilling from the moment she took multiple keys to her walkup from a fragrant purse.) Later still, I would have said yes to the newspaper job in the West. And after that . . . And so the memory of the boat becomes an emblem of cowardice in my mind. I have a friend who calls himself a coward because, a decorated veteran, he once froze under fire in combat. Now, that is a memory and that is a cowardice I would love to have in my past (long in my past). As it was, I failed to get into a boat, and I think of things undone.

It is probably true that most of us regret such things more than palpable mistakes (though to say this may only be to say we have been lucky, or even prudent). If we are very unlucky—live long enough—we come to that catastrophic moment that in fact changes things utterly. A tragic accident, a betrayal, a diagnosis. I can remember twice when I neglected to see an oncoming car at an intersection and could have been dead in an instant. Once as a youth "playing with guns" I could have shot a friend. The surprising bullet went over his head. But if we dance out of tragedy's way, we have those memories of moments when we might have done something that set us on a different, better path. And what held one back? The cowardice that endures is that hesitation that prevents me from the gesture or the sentence that puts the self at risk, but might free it too. The word or deed that might have mattered to someone. T. S. Eliot had incantatory words for this: "between the emotion and the response falls the shadow." So many emotions. So many shadows.

As to memoir—I take the purist view myself, and have little patience for inaccuracy. But getting the facts right is the least of the problem. There is a paradox at the heart of memoir. Probably no recent memoirist has had such a thorough—or at least such an explicit—grasp of the hazards of the form as has Dave Eggers. In his book *A Heartbreaking Work of Staggering Genius*, Eggers describes the tragedy of his young adulthood: he lost both his parents within a couple of months of each other, and, at age twenty-one, he inherited the care of a brother who was then just eight years old. The center of the book recounts how the two survived, in sometimes comic and always affecting prose. The story would have been quite enough for me. But it was not enough for Eggers. The book is preceded by a sort of essay/collage that provides a meta-view of the work, in which the author scrupulously (one is asked to believe) acknowledges his departures from fact, then examines and questions, even mocks his motives and methods. "While the author is self-conscious about being self-referential, he is also knowing about this self-conscious self-referentiality," Eggers writes. "Further . . . he also plans to be clearly, obviously aware of his knowingness about his self-consciousness of self-referentiality. Further . . . "

Eggers knows that there is no escape from this endless Morton Salt–box regression of self-absorption, and the comic confession works to inoculate him against the charge all memoirists must fear, that of narcissism. But the problem is larger than narcissism. When self-presentation is the enterprise, "accuracy" is impossible. All narrative bears at most a partial relation to the truth, and personal narrative must be the most partial of all, if only because the author knows all too much about his subject. No word in English is more likely than "I" to precede a lie, and if the subject is complicated at all, that pronoun must almost without fail precede a half-truth. We have all been stopped by those Ancient Mariners—in life, not only in print—who have understood their own lives all too well. For them, they are their addiction, or their abuse, or their triumph over this to become that, and their tales obscure the person on whom they shine such light. I sometimes want to tell these self-analysts impatiently, "No, you don't know the half of it, you are more, you are more." There is a reason that Henry Adams wrote his

Education in the third person, an effort to acknowledge the separate self observing the self. (This is a trick, of course, that can't be repeated by many others, for most of whom it would lead irretrievably to comedy.) The dilemma is inescapable and really it needn't be escaped. But all memoir is at its heart fictive.

4. Self and Selves

F. SCOTT FITZGERALD, for whom romance illuminated most observation, wrote that "personality is an unbroken string of successful gestures." We may (especially when we're young) find this idea kind of attractive, exciting in its suggestion of self-creation. Personality in this sense is a willed act, and indeed it is an *act*. On the other hand, this self-generating self places a lot of power in the hands of others. Gestures, after all, are purely social things. Since one can't make them to oneself, personality then depends on an audience.

I try now to think of an unbroken string of my own successful gestures. I do come up with an instance, in which I succeeded in creating myself (for an audience of one) as a perfectly coherent figure. As it happens, this memory is not a pleasant sensation, since the figure I created was that of a drunken, lecherous, pious hypocrite. I achieved this in the eyes of a fellow about my age (we were then in our mid-thirties) in the course of just a few weeks, during which time I flirted merrily with his wife, appeared late and unsteadily at his door, and lost his cat. The last two events may have been one; I recall only chasing the cat loudly through his neighborhood in the dark as he begged me to stop. In any case, the next time he saw me I was on my knees in prayer in the giant nave of Trinity Church in Boston, my wife and little daughters beside me, at a Christmas Eve service. He and his family were in the pew behind. I can feel now his eyes on the back of my neck. We did not really know each other and this was all he had ever seen of me, but he thought he knew quite enough, and who could blame him? I can only hope that the moment afforded him the pleasure that such uncomplicated contempt can occasionally bring to us all.

Rarely do we achieve such a completeness in the eyes of others. I have done worse than make overtures to that pretty, gray-eyed woman. But generally one's sins get diluted slightly by some mitigating act. Perhaps there is someone to whom I have been without exception kind and selfless, though this person is not coming as quickly to mind. Don't we generally stumble through life as ambiguous to others as we are to ourselves? Always hoping that they will assemble a portrait that in some way accords with our idealized (or at least compassionately understood) self. Multiple eyes gaze upon you—and in a lifetime of scrutiny from different angles, you are held up and turned in the light like a semiprecious stone, or perhaps a piece of fool's gold, and over the years if not by one set of eyes but by all together your flaws are seen and your worth assayed.

And is that it? Are we the sum of people's conceptions of us? I can remember the actual moment this thought first came to me, in English class at college. I can see the very classroom—it was such a bold, such a nicely scary little idea (Who am I? . . . There is no I!) that it caused a frisson and the moment stuck in mind. In recent years it has become fashionable to give this "idea"—really a sensation that must have occurred to generations of sophomores—a language, a depth, a status as a postmodern concept, that the self (like everything else these days that is not sheer rock) is really a "social construct." Race and gender, long seeming to be rudimentary building blocks of identity, are themselves "problematized." If you have to reckon with the arbitrariness of calling yourself a man or woman, it begins to seem really perilous to get more specific than that.

And yet all the while the suspicion lurks that there is some inner self that needs to be known—discovered even, and then obeyed, and served. It is like a belief in the future: an utter certainty and an ever-receding illusion.

We have a hedged and provisional sense of the self now, and I find it interesting to think of this next to the folk wisdom that governed my upbringing. "He's a Todd. Just like his father. Is that not exactly like a Townsley, though? He's got his mother's stubborn streak, I'll tell you that." Tradition thinks that we have a self inborn, a "nature"—and part of me still thinks that. Where would Greek tragedy be if everything were left to "nurture"? It's a suspicion that can get out of hand though—at the extreme it can lead you to confuse mind with knowledge. I have caused myself a great deal of unnecessary trouble by thinking that there are some things that I don't need to learn, knowing them as I must innately.

The concept of personality is a relatively new one, emerging—or getting a name—only in the late nineteenth century. Previously, people were inclined to speak of character. A protean quality is inherent in personality; consistency is the hallmark of character. Character is built (slowly, out of great marble blocks of deeds laid carefully upon one another); personality can be invented. Or can it? They say that among victims of Alzheimer's and other dementias it is personality—or at least the gestures by which we know it— that is the last thing to go. And it is true that when you find yourself in some unusual situation something essential does seem to emerge; in army basic training, I was the shy but obedient, bookish boy I had been in grade school. Character and personality have this in common: they describe how we are known to others. Identity is how we are known to ourselves. You hope you have good character, and if you do you probably think more about its failures than its successes, so along with it goes a certain constant low-level suffering. It is probably foolish to think of your personality at all. Only Miss America contestants can do so with confidence. People try, though, for some reason, happy to place themselves on grids and scales and willing to take their Myers-Briggs test results as definitive. The question that plagues us, even if we are unaware, is not how others know us but how we know ourselves. It is the unicorn in the glass.

To thine own self be true. In *Sincerity and Authenticity*, Lionel Trilling calls attention to that familiar passage in *Hamlet*: Polonius's speech of advice. "Neither a borrower . . ." and so forth. The speech is famously comic. In fact, it is so famous that it's hard to know how comic it really is. We have been heavily educated to think it funny, and its actors invariably prompt us with broad gestures, and the laughter is automatic. But Trilling's point is not about the speech as a whole but about the last two lines: "To thine own self be true, and it doth follow, as the night the day, thou canst not then be false to any man." However the scene is played, Trilling argues, these lines are different from the rest. Try as we may, we can't hear the advice as silly or sententious. "Our impulse to make its sense consistent with our general view of Polonius is defeated by the way the lines sound, by their lucid moral lyricism. He has conceived of sincerity as an essential condition of virtue and has discovered how it is to be attained."

But if only it were so easy! As Trilling goes on to remark, the lines touch a great longing—"what a promise the phrase sings to our ears!"—but they also pose a great challenge. What is the "true self"? How do you find it? He cites the Matthew Arnold lines:

Below the surface-stream, shallow and light
Of what we say we feel—below the stream,
As light, of what we think we feel—there flows
With noiseless current strong, obscure and deep,
The central stream of what we feel indeed.

"The Matthew Arnold lines," I say as if everyone knew them. I didn't know them before reading them in Trilling, and in truth they don't number among the poet's best. "What we feel indeed." Good God—with that gentle image of deep currents Arnold seems to suggest it's not much work to get down into what we know instead to be the turgid muck of the unconscious. Can anyone live down there? Could the world tolerate anyone who did? Maybe Polonius's lines, in a more profound way than the rest of his speech, are comic after all.

And yet I am stalked by the idea that somewhere, beneath the surface of something—whatever the image, the preposition is always "beneath"—there lies a stable and unadulterated self. Has one not had glimpses of him? Have we not all done something instinctual that seems to reveal something essential about us? (Years ago in a dormitory shower room, I intervene in a fight. "Hey. Stop picking on my friend." The bully stops. I feel that I have spoken from the core, that I have some moral identity!)

My friend Margaret Bullitt-Jonas knows the problem I am turning over in my mind. Margaret, an Episcopal priest and an author, offers me a quotation from Thomas Merton:

We are at liberty to be real, or to be unreal. We may be true or false, the choice is ours. We may now wear one mask and now another, and never, if we so desire, appear with our own true face. But we cannot make these choices with impunity. Causes have effects, and if we lie to ourselves and to others, then we cannot expect to find truth and reality whenever we happen to want them. If we have chosen the way of falsity we must not be surprised that truth eludes us when we finally come to need it.

This passage may lack "lucid moral lyricism," but nonetheless it seems to contain the wisdom of the ages, and does so with the force of the pulpit. It stirs remorse. It dares me to think in shame of an infinity of fraudulent moments: the false laugh, the swallowed opinion, the sycophant's praise—or, worse, the bullying of certitude, the unguent of willed charm. Company courtier, cultural bureaucrat, hedger of true feelings. Away with these masks. Let me be one person for everyone, and let that person be who I really am. Ah . . . but who is that? And then quickly the passage curdles in my mind. In all its pious tautology it is beyond unsatisfying. I get peevish about it, annoyed. What is my "true self" and who is Thomas Merton to be so sure I've got one?

I mention this succession of thoughts to my friend, and her response, seemingly offhand, contains more wisdom than Merton's injunction. "I wonder if being authentic means recognizing the many selves within the self. Listening to them," she adds, "but learning which ones are worth paying attention to . . ." This does seem to me to get closer to the truth.

Perhaps "masks" are not the problem at all. Oscar Wilde mischievously (but maybe accurately?) said, "Man is least himself when he talks in his own person. Give him a mask and he will tell you the truth." Would it dismay me to learn that Margaret's open countenance was actually masklike, that her direct and unembarrassed speech hid a reticent other-self? No, on the contrary, I think it would only enhance her in my estimation. Good cheer is almost by definition a mask, and it's one that I pretty reliably wear, and I hate to feel it fall.

We harbor selves that go deeper than masks. They are not something we don. They are creatures with agendas of their own. All the selves that have lived within me; I wish sometimes they could be tossed aside but they are real.

There ought to be a church into which one could slip, with a cleric on duty who was interested in neither mortal nor venial sins but in confusion and misperception. The Church of Seeing Clearly. And in that murmurous confessional box one could find forgiveness for the behavior of all those errant other selves that inhabit one's skin. Father, I have been blinded by language. Father, I have been a snob. Father, I have had too much to drink.

For much of my life, for instance, I think it seemed to me the world was made of words. How pleasing it was as a child to feel the words accrue like interest. I loved standardized tests. If only life were a multiple-choice exam. What is a fortnight? What is the meaning of "yclept"? What word is most nearly the opposite of "salient"? Oar is to water as . . . (a) sail is to wind, (b) pilot is to plane, (c) propeller is to air, (d) wheel is to wagon.

The first real interest I had outside of books was sailing, and at first, I think, it was the language as much as the sport that appealed to me, though at last I found pleasure in the undescribed sea. The difference between sloop and cutter, ketch and yawl. Snatch blocks, turnbuckles, running backstays, genoa, and mizzen, sheets and halyards and the dinghy's painter, the bowline and clove hitch. I didn't understand the irony of my yachtsman host (my classmate's father) when I would sail on his cruising boat. He called me Professor. Children should beware when adults call them names like that. I realized only in retrospect what a twit he must have thought me, and though I also realized that he himself was not the jolly fellow he seemed, he had my number. I struggle now to see beyond language, but for a long time didn't even make the effort. College was little help. Fleeing from science I couldn't understand and history that bored me, I took refuge in poems and novels, and there was plenty of refuge to be taken. As if Marvell, Wordsworth, T. S. Eliot were not enough to cloud the mind, there came from the other direction the astringent sensibility of logical positivism, which suggested that indeed there was no such thing as an understanding separate from one's ability to articulate it in language. This doctrine came to seem to me worthy as a discipline, not as a faith, but the inexpressible remained deeply suspect. (Sex at last chipped away at this view.)

Words unlock the world, but then if you are not careful they put you behind bars of their own. I am still a querulous, finicky listener, defensive against excess, and I sometimes realize that this very wariness makes me resist that which another part of the heart wants to hear, the direct cry of belief. The language of politics—the language of commitment generally—was off-limits, embarrassing. This was especially true of the language of protest—"Make love, not war"— and thus I found myself politically disengaged, out of, I now think, not genuine skepticism but an excessive delicacy. How often has simple squeamishness made me deaf to people who should have been heard? I resist the easy distinction between "style" and "substance," and think it is right to do so. But at some moment you realize that there is a meaning that can be felt in the most imprecise language like a child's clumsy kiss.

There is a habit of self-presentation among the intellectual and reasonably prosperous classes, who like to speak of their humble, especially their ethnic origins. About their Jewish or Catholic or even Presbyterian guilt—every religion seems to think it has a corner on guilt-induction—or their limited cultural inheritance. No books in the house, no music, no cuisine. With the TV and mac-and-cheese that was their usual fare, they're not villainous, just limited families. These childhoods for the intellectual classes are the cultural counterparts of rags-to-riches accounts one hears from "self-made" executives or entrepreneurs. Hard work and native wit got me where I am—got me tenure, got me the corner office—that's the implicit lesson. I am without provenance. I came from nowhere!

I have never been able to take part in this performance, but not because my origins were grand. To do so would be to feel an unbearable sense of betrayal of my parents. Class meant so very much to them. Their solidarity was always upwards, and I absorbed their feelings. Now it strikes me that I may be about to betray them anyway, if I try to lay my snobbish sins at their feet.

In any case, I cannot talk easily about my humble roots, even when I suspect that they were, in various ways, humbler than the roots of those who quote their grandmother's Russian proverbs. In an odd inversion, people who remain silent in these situations are felt to be discreetly modest about their privileged youth. In part for this reason, most people meeting me think that I am an old rich kid, probably (if they were pressed to think about it) the son of a corporate lawyer or something similar. I have been asked sometimes where I went to boarding school, often by people who went to one themselves. And they have a point. I was raised to be a rich kid, only without the complication of money.

I remember taking the train to the city, the summer before I went off to college, to meet my father for lunch at the Stork Club, a place neither one of us had any business being. Afterward, he bought me some of their famous Cub Room aftershave. Not without some pride, I took it with me to freshman year. When my choice of school had been announced that spring a snippy friend of my mother said to her, "Well, that's a snob school, you know." And my mother—it is one of my fondest memories of her—replied, "That's good, because my son is a snob."

Wherever it came from, I imputed wonderful things to the upper classes and was a student of their ways. Nice people eat asparagus with their fingers, and call patios terraces, and say "great fun" a lot. Images from my young-adult years can still resonate, stirring in me that remembered sense of a world of superior grace out there somewhere. I remember the first time I saw Cambridge, Massachusetts (and the ultimate "snob school"), and there were student cars, MGs and Jaguars, parked rakishly, half on the sidewalk, outside Adams House. I remember anchor lights reflected in the rippled night water of Edgartown harbor. A tiny pink bow at the top of a bra just glimpse-able beneath the neckline of my partner's dress, at a yacht club dance. A Park Avenue apartment ("apartment" a word that had once seemed akin to "tenement")—its walnut-paneled rooms stretching down an endless corridor.

Once I went to a coming-out party at the Rainbow Room for the daughter of one of America's richest families. (I was sneaked in by a classmate who by virtue of his birth deserved to be there.) I remember (besides my blazing cheeks) chiefly a sense of disillusionment. It was the toasting that did it. The brother of the debutante got up and spoke about how nervous she had been that day, how many cigarettes she had smoked. This in my innocence seemed terribly coarse.

"Let me tell you about the very rich. They are different from you and me." I thought so, and wanted to think so. Fitzgerald's remark is seldom quoted without Hemingway's put-down: "Yes. They have more money." Fitzgerald, in less-remembered words, went on about the rich, saying: they are "soft where we are hard, and cynical where we are trustful . . ." This for a time became my view, too, and if it fails to be comprehensively fair it puts a nice edge on that mixture of awe and resentment that many of the rest of us feel toward our presumed betters.

But a fascination with wealth and class is all in the end a form of romance. On the whole, I think romantic notions of aristocracy may be healthier than those about the nobility of the poor—I have suffered from that fallacy, too, but less persistently—because the disappointment that the upper class provides is its own consolation. Mercifully, in recent years we have had a parade of such outlandish miscreants of great wealth that any association between fortune and style seems to have been washed away forever. But it took me an inordinate amount of time to recognize the utter randomness with which decency, like raisins in a cake, is distributed throughout the social classes, and I can't forget that sense of upward yearning. I think back with affection to my mother. One day after she had been widowed, I took her to lunch at the Ritz bar in Boston, with its lovely winter view of the bare tangled trees of the Public Garden. Outside the tinted window a man passed by wearing a Chesterfield coat. Later she would recall the day and "that man in the Chesterfield coat." I think it was one of the nicest things I ever did for her.

The Ritz . . . the Ritz . . . scene, in Shakespeare's phrase, of "my dear time's waste." A boss of mine, a longtime journalist, once said that he didn't trust a man who didn't drink.

(Obviously, he felt correctly that he could trust me.) I recognized the remark to be outrageous but it didn't feel outrageous, because I, like him, followed the Drinking Man's Code. It was not all that rare in the second half of the last century (and long before that, too, I imagine), prevalent especially among men of Irish and English descent. The code—never truly articulated, of course—held that drink was the one weakness allowable to a man. And done correctly it was not really a weakness at all. My father taught me an early contempt for anyone who could not "hold his liquor," and the corollary admiration for the man who could "really put it away" and not show it. There was to be no concern about abusing your body, or cutting yourself off from your own feelings, or any of that—any amount of drink was okay as long as you didn't get "sloppy." There was a certain inevitable tension here—surely the point of drinking was to alter your mind in some way, and yet the changes had to be invisible. "Hold your liquor" turned out to be a rather fungible rule. Well before you staggered, raised your voice, grew violent, it could become clear that it was your liquor that was holding you. And I finally understood the essential paradox of drink, that it lets you feel closer to others, while they feel further from you.

But drink was a sacrament and a medicine, it was lubricant and fuel. Drink appeared to be very nearly what made it possible to be a man, and it was your reward for being one.

There was much that was unallowed to men: tears, anger, sorrow, glee—any excess of emotion, really. Drink took the place of these, and to the drinking man it seemed a perfectly good deal.

I have a therapist friend who points out that "one cannot avoid pain, one can only avoid the pain that comes from trying to avoid pain." To live that way, avoiding pain, would be to leave many bottles unopened and to leave unused, like a closetful of clothes, many emotional costumes. Always sober, in a denim personality, one would face the world without artifice. I am not sure how appealing this is, to be honest, but yes indeed, I have fled, and do flee, from pain that might have been instructive. How much one's crutches become one's nature.

In my thirties I was a Ritz regular, where it was normal for people like me to have a martini (on the rocks with a twist) before lunch. And maybe another? Or maybe just a "small carafe" of wine, or on a special day, another martini and then a carafe, and then perhaps another one of those? Then back to work a little merrier, to make the difficult phone calls one had put off during the morning. By the end of that decade I was behaving in a way that later or in other settings would have certified me worthy of rehab—the notion of lunch without a drink became very unpleasant and on some days insupportable, and a long road trip presumed the comfort of a companionable six-pack. But then again a lot of other people were behaving that way too, and whether for good or ill I eluded diagnosis.

Something more like decorum prevails now in my life, the gin untouched for years, only wine, and seldom at lunch. "Societal influence" gets a very bad reputation, but I owe it something. I profited when it became generally unacceptable for an office in the afternoon to be full of men (and the occasional woman) pretending to be sober. It is nice to think of my own easing into moderation as a matter of maturity and self-control. But the Age of Chardonnay deserves a lot of credit.

Still, you know, he's always with you, the drinking man; and even if it is chardonnay, he knows where his next drink is coming from and when it will arrive.

"The quality of despair is precisely this: it is unaware of being despair," said Kierkegaard. It strikes me now that many of my selves have given a lot of energy to avoiding that knowledge. The figures I have sketched above, drunk on words, drunk on class, or merely drunk—these people shadow me. I try to give them the slip but know that I will never lose them entirely. They are craftsmen of a sort, masons, to be exact, each gifted in building walls, less than clear about what they are walling out.

When I can get rid of my old friends, there is a fellow I keep beckoning back. He is hard to name, but he is occasionally capable of self-forgetfulness. He sees the world not in a hierarchy of status but of virtue. He tells himself the truth and tries not to lie to others. Despite a congenital difficulty in expressing affection, he somehow makes people closest to him understand that he loves them. He recognizes, in the light of all of human possibilities, how modest, even though elusive, these few virtues are.

Margaret speaks again: "I think that we may feel real in direct proportion to the reality that we can grant to others."

5. In the Moment

IN *SINCERITY AND AUTHENTICITY,* Trilling traces the notion of the authentic self in its literary and cultural antecedents. He argues that the idea of authenticity is essentially oppositional, a stance taken, a distinction achieved. With seeming finality Rousseau and the Romantic movement placed the individual and the society at odds. It became one of the great themes in Western culture: that which is native, true, unaffected, pure—all are threatened by falsity, oppression of convention, and the social order. It was natural, even reflexive, for artists to celebrate the individual, and a significant strain in literature devoted itself to separating sheep from goats: the "authentic" hero from the crowd. Literature seen this way is an extended sermon on the perils of inauthenticity. Trilling remarks that it became a function of art to "teach . . . readers who they are not to be if they really wish to *be.* It is easy at least to understand how not to be: we must not be like anyone else."

Put this way, the dead-endedness of the concept is plain. Yet you cannot deny its centrality to our culture, to our lives. No one can escape, no one wants to escape this longing for distinction. It would be foolish to pretend otherwise. For all the lip service we pay to the great universal truths, we do not like to think of ourselves as universal but as unique. That part of ourselves that we tend to value is the part that is distinct. We flail about not wanting to slip below the waters of sameness.

Trilling writes chiefly about the tradition of English and Continental writing, about Flaubert, Conrad, and (most interestingly) Jane Austen. Austen, novelist of manners, nonetheless created a species of authentic hero and heroine, who distinguished themselves by superior intelligence and delicacy of feeling.

But the great voices of the American past similarly sound the theme of an independent, even defiant selfhood, if in a more robust and spirited way. And who can or would want to resist it? True, the idea of millions of readers imagining that they too are marching to a different drummer has an inherent poignancy. But who would abjure the call toward courage of mind from Melville in his great chapter "The Lee Shore": "As in landlessness alone resides the highest truth, shoreless, indefinite as God—so, better to perish is it in that howling infinite, than be ingloriously dashed upon the lee, even if that were safety!"

And I cannot, still, read these lines from Emerson without feeling stirred:

"Trust thyself. Every heart vibrates to that iron string."

"Envy is ignorance . . . Imitation is suicide."

And (on spouters of received wisdom): "Conformity makes them not false in a few particulars, authors of a few lies, but false in all particulars. Their every truth is not quite true. Their two is not the real two, their four not the real four; so that every word they say chagrins us, and we know not where to begin to set them right. . . . "

Emerson knew his country. He knew it was a lonely place and that its citizens fled from loneliness into the complacency of the herd, and the herd ever swelled. He can be misread, I think, as a prophet of heedless individualism, but what he celebrates and stirs instead is that core of identity that at our best moments we feel we can touch. The title of the essay was not "Self-Invention," but "Self-Reliance."

By the mid-twentieth century in America, the idea that damage was done to the human spirit by society was an institutionalized way of thinking. Everyone feared being a member of the "Lonely Crowd," forsaking individual initiative for "other-directedness." Marxist wisdom, defanged, held that democratic capitalism had separated "man" (as was still said then) from himself. Alienation was so central a concept to intellectual life that someone suggested that the *Partisan Review* had special typewriters with a key that could type the word at a single stroke.

Lionel Trilling was scarcely an apologist for the state or for convention, nor was he dismissive of the psychological state that provoked a hunger for authenticity. But he was suspicious of the quest nonetheless. There was an even larger case to be made against the whole notion of authenticity. As argued by Theodor Adorno and his fellow political theorists of the Frankfurt School, the concept was a vain and arrogant attempt to escape history itself, a failure to recognize that we are not the creatures of will we may suppose, but creations of the past. Trilling confined himself to art. He had droll words for those readers and museumgoers and theatergoers who willingly accept the flagellation of modern art—"in the registration of oneself in the company of those who, because they see themselves as damned, are saved."

For Trilling, the "fallen state" was more nearly a continuing descent, and it had become a descent literally into madness. Alienation itself became a route to selfhood. Writing in the late sixties, Trilling dwelt on the then modish theories of R. D. Laing and Norman O. Brown, prophets of the cult of inspired derangement. Trilling says of their readers, "Many among us find it gratifying to entertain the thought that alienation is overcome only by the completeness of alienation, and that alienation completed is not a deprivation or depletion but a potency."

We stepped back from that brink. The thinkers who

seemed so dangerous to Trilling faded in the public imagination soon after he wrote. But we have nonetheless lived in the condition he described. The flirtation with madness may have passed, but the long romance with the created heroic, authentic self flourishes.

"Existence precedes essence" were the heady words of my youth, Sartre's existential self. Did anyone I ever met quite believe it? I remember the girl in black who used to hang out on campus, violating parietal rules, and her similarly dressed boyfriend: this was before the whole East Coast dressed in black. Did they really smoke Gauloises? That's my memory. Existentialism was a great argument for sex, it was true. Really, I have no business writing of Sartre. My eyes bounced off the page when I first tried to read him, and I have never found him congenial. He gave us one of the ugliest short sentences of his century: "Hell is other people." Sartre asked us to see the alienation of modern man in the plight of the waiter who had forsaken his identity for the ceremonies of his role. I resisted and do resist— my sympathies went to the waiter, whom he portrayed (in *Being and Nothingness*) as the very embodiment of inauthenticity. The poor guy, I thought: he was doing his job. I don't remember any long nights of terrifying freedom perched on the abyss of anything. But I was slow to recognize something: how the challenge—to create yourself, to be yourself—hung in the air over all of us. It hangs there still. I take it to be true that even for people who have never heard of Jean-Paul Sartre, the culture is haunted by the existential invitation.

Big ideas have a hazardous life in America. They are subject to being stolen, counterfeited, sold on the street like fake Rolexes. Frank Lloyd Wright tries to create an architecture to complement the prairie, and his followers give us acres of ranch houses with picture windows. We have, I think, a popular American existentialism, which is Sartre without politics, Kierkegaard's leap without the faith. (Who teaches all those young athletes to say that they can be whatever they want to be?) What is the vast self-help industry but a vulgar existentialism, the wine cooler of the people?

Book after book speaks of slipping out of the husk of your old life and blooming anew. A current, hugely popular, and particularly bizarre one, *The Secret,* tells us that we can think our way to success through a mystical alliance of self-creators. "Like thoughts attract like thoughts" is the basic idea: "You are a creator and there is an easy process to create using the law of attraction." Then, I guess (to be strictly accurate I didn't get all the way through the book)—I guess these people are going to converge like souls called together in the Rapture. Just do it. (Or don't even do it, think it.) Another author, Eckhart Tolle, outlines the secret of "awakening to your life's purpose" in his book *A New Earth.* The place of the title is not a physical place or a new social contract; it is a state of awareness. It is not, Tolle stresses, a utopia, because utopias can happen only in the future, and the only reality worth thinking about is the now. But thinking is very much the wrong word. Your presence in the new earth is achieved by loss of ego, or by "learning to escape from incessant and compulsive thinking." This isn't the first time that people have been urged to lose their minds. But thought as a looming threat to the American citizen—now, *that* seems an odd idea nonetheless.

One can argue that self-invention has been with us from the start of our history, but it lately seems to have taken on a mean, even nihilistic edge. Our heroes have often started over or arisen from nowhere, but traditionally they have not been so pleased with themselves as today's auto-creators.

Now comes before the late-night television interviewer the actor who has a new and "daring" film to promote. Why did you take this chance? he is asked. "I was too comfortable," he replies. "I don't like comfort." It is an answer à la mode. We are expected to approve. He's taking chances, and making himself up with every film. Fleeing comfort, seeking the edge. Of course, the man has so much money and adulation that you wonder what it would take to make him uncomfortable. Probably he would have to hire a professional torturer. Comfort doesn't sound so bad to me. The demons at bay? What's wrong with that? Even in art comfort has its advantages: the reassurance of form and symmetry. But the actor knows better, and with this dialogue he presents himself as a self-creator.

And here come the billionaires, quoted in the *New York Times*, speaking of the feats of self-invention they have accomplished. Says the cable television entrepreneur, "I think there are people, including myself at certain times in my career, who because of their uniqueness warrant whatever the market will bear." The blind gracelessness of the self-made man.

Still, there is power and allure in the notion of self-creation. It is more than starry optimism, or the cynical merchandising of a "new you." It has become a secular religion with us, a sustaining belief. A psychiatrist friend of mine puts me onto a book, now obscure but once, he points out, quite influential in the field. It is called *The Search for Authenticity*, by J. F. T. Bugental, published in 1965. I look for it. It turns out to be one of those valuable documents that codify the wisdom of an age—an age that is still very much with us. Bugental attempted to delineate the concept of the Authentic Self—secular, apolitical, amoral—and though he himself may not be widely remembered, his language permeates our sensibilities. The figure he helped to define has been for the past half century a *beau ideal*.

Although authenticity is a concept at the center of his work, Bugental struggles with a definition. "By authenticity, I mean a central genuineness and awareness of being.

Authenticity is that presence of an individual in his living in which he is fully aware in the present moment, in the present situation. Authenticity is difficult to convey in words, but experientially it is readily perceived in our self or in others."

Hmm. We do indeed recognize this language, and recognize it in part because of its imprecision. But here is further, better, Bugental: "The authentic person is broadly aware of himself, his relationships, and his world in all dimensions . . . accepts that decisions are the very stuff of living . . . takes responsibility for his decisions. . . . It is here that the terrible threat of authenticity lies."

There is something gravely exciting about all of this, especially the "terrible threat." Much is risked, the loosening of familiar ties, the comforts of old habits and neuroses, but much is to be gained in freedom you have never before known. It's the swashbuckling attitude, partly, that is appealing: Bring it on! But also the promise of a sort of unity of being: "Awareness is always feelingful awareness," Bugental says, "all the senses involved, not just cognitive."

This prescription for living, though it seeks to create the self, calls into question the very idea of self, as the author is fully aware. The self, insofar as it represents consistency, is the enemy of unfettered, in-the-moment response. Bugental wanted to get rid of the concept entirely, substituting for "self" the "I-process," a term that for obvious reasons didn't survive, but was meant to suggest the act of continuous choice and transformation. "What would it mean to be freed of the Self? It would mean living fully in each moment, dwelling on the 'razor's edge' of Now."

This is a call each of us hears. On the one hand, when people tell us to live in the moment, it seems to me to be something close to saying, "Cease to be human." To be human is to be conscious. And consciousness is about a remembered past and an imagined future. It is true that we have all known moments of joy, and a freedom from past and future has often been essential to those moments. (Alas, moments of rage and pain too.) Do we create ourselves at such times? Maybe we do, maybe we simply add a layer, like a coat of paint. Maybe we reveal ourselves instead. Do we want or need to live on the razor's edge?

The confession in the Book of Common Prayer is briskly inclusive: "We have left undone those things which we ought to have done, and we have done those things which we ought not to have done." That about covers the waterfront. When I say the Apostles' Creed to myself, sometimes I am scarcely aware of saying it, but sometimes I listen in wonder at what I feel compelled to recite. "He sitteth at the right hand of God the Father Almighty, whence he shall come to judge the living and the dead . . . the resurrection of the body . . . and the life everlasting. . . . " I realize that of the entire prayer I believe only a couple of lines—perhaps only one—with the force of faith: "the forgiveness of sins." It is the great central Christian doctrine, the virtue patented by Christianity, though I imagine practiced in no greater degree by Christians than by anyone else. One believes it only if one has experienced the miracle on earth. To have been forgiven is to feel what people must mean when they say they are in God's hands.

The last words Sir Walter Scott said to his son-in-law: "I may have but a minute to speak to you. My dear, be a good man—be virtuous, be religious, be a good man. Nothing else will give you comfort when you come to lie here."

Saul Bellow, in his ninetieth year, said to a friend, "Tell me, was I a mensch or a schmuck?"

There is a savage side to the created self. (It reminds us that there is power, even violence, in the root meaning of *authenticity*.) "Living in the moment" can be a summons to invention, but also to destruction. There is perhaps no more readily available mode of living on the edge than lying—and it is often an exciting form at that. Anyone who has ever lied for an extended time—who has "lived a lie"—knows something awful. It is something worse than guilt—guilt, after all, is a sign of conscience, of one's residual goodness. No, what one knows is the dark pleasure of the lie itself. Deception deceives the deceiver, and one way it does so is to impart a heightened sense of newness of self, the illusion of an outlaw transcendence.

When it is over—but is it ever over?—can you ever, then, tell the truth? No, not about the past. But when it is over, in the sense that you find yourself living in the lie-free present, you occasionally feel awash in gratitude, like a former addict, gratitude for whatever it is that prevents you from lying again, and like the addict you may become a scrupulous avoider of the poison.

Then it is a relief not to live in the moment but in a coherence of time, stretching backward and forward: to live, that is, in a life. Surely this is a sounder meaning of authenticity—a life that can accommodate itself in its entirety. It is of course an impossible goal as an absolute. "Humankind cannot bear very much reality," and learning to forget may be as necessary as learning to remember. Yet the effort to achieve some capaciousness for our warring parts leads inexorably to the other virtue that Eliot celebrated in "The Four Quartets": "The only wisdom we can hope to acquire/is the wisdom of humility: humility is endless."

"Living in the moment" becomes, the more one thinks about it, a shabby phrase. But there is a very particular sense in which it represents wisdom. Not to be yourself, but to *see* yourself as you are in the present, unredeemed by acts past or future: that knowledge opens an avenue to moral clarity. Lionel Trilling points this out, curiously enough in an instance from Jane Austen, not a writer one thinks of as "existential." He suggests that the code of *Mansfield Park* is exactly the realism implied by seeing oneself clearly *right now*. "It is in the exigent present that things are what they really are, not in the unfolding future." This way lies pain, no doubt, but also perhaps a kind of freedom, if only the freedom of brass tacks. You are unburdened of the slyly degrading search for justification in your past, the dreamy erasure of today's sins by tomorrow's intended good deeds. I sit here on a winter afternoon, struggling for exactness, and I know exactly when I falter.

A rigorous and unassailable code, but there are corollaries and codicils even to it, I think. The stark judgment of the moment is a rigor meant for oneself alone, not for others. Basic human decency argues against it. What we mean by compassion is often just that sympathetic imagination for how people got where they are, and that belief in their possibilities for change. And there is another caveat: occasionally we do grant to ourselves, having felt some mercy from a source unknown, the possibility of redemption.

I turn one last time to my wise friend Margaret, but this time her truth must disappoint me, because it depends on that which so many of us don't quite have, an all-informing faith. "I wonder how," she says, "the sense of lost authenticity relates to the spiritual hunger to know why we are here. There is a kind of teleology to being authentic: we are authentic when we are being true to our real nature and our real purpose in life. . . . I am being authentic when I am open to God, praising God, serving God."

6. One's Fate

I SUPPOSE WE ASK too much of love. For more than a hundred years we have been the children of Matthew Arnold, standing above Dover Beach. I think of that vivid poem and it's almost as if I can hear the waves grinding the rocks on the shore. "Ah, love, let us be true / To one another! . . . Nor certitude, nor peace, nor help from pain; . . . Where ignorant armies clash by night."

Inward, inward we turn, away from the world.

We ask too much of love—but surprisingly love often delivers.

Wood, field, house, food and drink, quirky, loyal friends, thoughts, endlessly amusing children, an endlessly mysterious and beautiful wife . . . "Love your fate," says Nietzsche. Who could do other than love mine? Yet a disconcerting thing: no story gets me here. What is the plot? For most of us, I think, life is a set of episodes, a vast off-the-books accounting that has little to do with sustained narrative. And how many of those moments—the most vivid, really, speaking strictly for myself—how many of them defeat one's sense of well-being! I am not sure it would be vastly different if I were looking back at an unbroken string of victories. The feeling I am trying to describe has little if anything to do with victory. Those who regularly triumph assure us that victory, too, pales and seems finally unsatisfying.

Together we sometimes consider the mystery of the long marriage. Not the central mystery, not the way passion deepens. A long-honored reticence prevents that. And not the shifting cargo of emotions, the angers, sorrows, and joys that this seemingly fragile vessel has contained. (Though doubtless all of these are the unspoken text.) But no, none of that is mentioned, just the everyday wonder of this self-renewing life.

It was once suggested (by me) that the most important element in marriage is politeness. Treat your spouse as well as you would treat a stranger and you are on the road to bliss. It was countered (by her): "Yes, I think if you can be married to someone, you can be married to anyone." A long-standing joke. It amuses me, because I think she is saying that she understands full well that her husband could be married to exactly one person. We have a life not very well recorded, though the album of great occasions always seems beside the point. The great occasions are every day, and they are fleeting and ephemeral, and yet they accumulate.

The girls will soon be home. We speak of them, the

unexpected blessing of "grown children." The professor, the editor, the consultant. Some would call them women but others take the long view, and the faces and gestures slide, as if with a will of their own, back and forth in time. They seem to have remained in character all these years, though no one could deny that they have now grown deeply beautiful. Very like women, it is true.

I am not alone in the following experience, I know; it happens to many in many happy places. Some gloom or other fills the inner space, behind the rib cage, but when I speak, my voice conveys something else altogether, some unexpected merriment. It is answered immediately in kind. Has she too been concealing woe, only to emit joy? And so, as it has for times beyond counting, newness enters the room. We are making this stuff up, of course, but why does it seem so real? Dialogue is the blessed freedom from the endless internal soliloquy. She becomes someone she has not been for half a lifetime or never been before. Is this dishonest? Should we share our "real feelings"? But our real feelings have reinvented themselves. Hypocrisy? If so, it is a grand and redemptive hypocrisy. It is a gift.

Where do they come from, these gifts? How resistant I am to the unseen! Others are on better terms with it; in the end we must all succumb to mystery. But I think within these sheltering walls I may sometimes understand another meaning of what it can be to "live in the moment." Not that striving, self-forging, abyss-staring quest—not that at all, but instead something more like acceptance. It happens perhaps at a table at night with the closest people and you feel not unpleasantly that you are no more or less real than the candlelight. That they have your substance, your very self, in their hands. That it is their gaze and their laughter, their unspoken and inexplicable affection that give you substance, that you are held there like a fallen leaf on an invisible updraft of air.

Acknowledgments

This book would not have been written without the encouragement, guidance, and patience of Betsy Lerner.

I am grateful to the staff of Riverhead Books, present and former—to Cindy Spiegel for her initial enthusiasm, to her successor, Geoffrey Kloske, and to Jake Morrissey and Sarah Bowlin.

Deborah Way provided essential help with research.

I acknowledge with thanks a grant from the National Trust for Historic Preservation.

Over the years I have had the great pleasure of working, on both sides of the desk, with many talented magazine editors, more than can be mentioned here. But the following may recognize their various kindnesses reflected in this book: Nelson Aldrich, Jane Berentson, James Conaway, Barry Estabrook, James R. Gaines, Alison Humes, Michael Janeway, Chris Jerome, Robert Manning, Cullen Murphy,

Daniel Okrent, Dean Robinson, Barbara Wallraff, William Whitworth, Susan Zesiger.

I am grateful for the encouragement of many friends, including Margaret Bullitt-Jonas and Robert Jonas, Jonathan Diamond, David Dorsey, Karyn Feiden, Dan Hall, Jonathan Harr, Alex and Becky Jacobson, Dr. David Kessler, Alex Kotlowitz, Adrian LeBlanc, Alan Lelchuk, John and Jan Maggs, Kevin Markey and Ann Hallock, Sean McPhetridge and Kirstin Mac Dougall, Catherine Newman, Robert and Kit Nylen, William and Marietta Pritchard, Carol and Larry Sheehan, Caroline Sly, David Sofield, Jack and Susan Walter, Mark Zenick, and my son-in-law, Liam Harte, and my aunt, Florence Chumas.

Thank you to Tracy Kidder for his robust and thoughtful reading of the manuscript and—infinitely more important—for decades of his generous friendship.

My sister-in-law, Mary Bagg, was a kind and meticulous reader of a draft of this book, and both she and her husband, Robert Bagg, have offered valuable criticism and support.

I owe much to my late teacher and lifelong friend Benjamin DeMott; had he survived to read it in manuscript, this would without doubt be a better book.

Possibly the most amiable literary community on earth is the Goucher College MFA program, under the direction of Patsy Sims, and I have benefited greatly from the friendship of my colleagues there and from that of the program's wonderful students.

At some moment, if you are lucky, a season turns and you discover that you are learning far more from your children than you ever taught them. That moment came for me, and it is impossible to express adequately my gratitude for the wisdom and love of my three daughters, Emily, Maisie, and Nell.

The adventure, possibility, and joy in my life I owe to Susan Bagg Todd. As for the problem that occupies these pages, she solved it long ago, in her own way, wordlessly.

Bibliography

Adomo, Theodor W. *The Jargon of Authenticity*. Evanston, IL: Northwestern University Press, 1973.

Appadurai, Arjun, ed. *The Social Life of Things: Commodities in Cultural Perspective*. Cambridge, UK: Cambridge University Press, 2006.

Banfield, Edward C. *The Democratic Muse: Visual Arts and the Public Interest*. New York: Basic Books, 1984.

Baudrillard, Jean. *America*. London: Verso, 1996.

Baudrillard, Jean. *The System of Objects*. London: Verso, 1996.

Beauty for America: Proceedings of the White House Conference on Natural Beauty. Washington, D.C.: U.S. Government Printing Office, 1965.

Benjamin, Walter. *Illuminations*. Hannah Arendt, ed. New York: Schocken Books, 1968.

Bockris, Victor. *Warhol*. Cambridge, MA: Da Capo Press, 2003.

Boorstin, Daniel J. *The Image: A Guide to Pseudo-Events in America*. New York: Harper & Row, 1961.

Botkin, Daniel B. *Discordant Harmonies: A New Ecology for the Twenty-first Century*. New York: Oxford University Press, 1990.

Bourdieu, Pierre. *Distinction: A Social Critique of the Judgement of Taste*. Trans. by Richard Nice. Cambridge, MA: Harvard University Press, 1996.

Brooks, David. *Bobos in Paradise: The New Upper Class and How They Got There*. New York: Simon & Schuster, 2000.

Bugental, J. F. T. *The Search for Authenticity*. New York: Holt, Rinehart and Winston, 1965.

Byrne, Rhonda. *The Secret*. New York: Atria Books, 2006.

Chase, Alston. *In a Dark Wood: The Fight Over Forests and the Rising Tyranny of Ecology*. Boston: Houghton Mifflin, 1995.

Cohen, Deborah. *Household Gods: The British and Their Possessions*. New Haven, CT: Yale University Press, 2006.

Cohen, Leah Hager. *Glass, Paper, Beans: Revelations on the Nature and Value of Ordinary Things*. New York: Doubleday, 1998.

Cronon, William. *Changes in the Land*. New York: Hill and Wang, 1985.

Cronon, William, ed. *Uncommon Ground: Toward Reinventing Nature*. New York: Norton, 1995.

Culler, Jonathan. *On Deconstruction*. Ithaca, NY: Cornell University Press, 1982.

Dominquez, Joe, and Vicki Robin. *Your Money or Your Life: Transforming Your Relationship with Money and Achieving Financial Independence*. New York: Penguin, 1997.

Eggers, David. *A Heartbreaking Work of Staggering Genius*. New York: Simon & Schuster, 2000.

Eisenberg, Evan. *The Ecology of Eden*. New York: Knopf, 1998.

Emerson, Ralph Waldo. Brooks Atkinson, ed. *The Selected Writings of Ralph Waldo Emerson*. New York: Random House, 1968.

Frank, Thomas, and Matt Weiland, eds. *Commodify Your Dissent: Salvos from The Baffler*. New York: Norton, 1997.

Gabler, Neal. *Life the Movie: How Entertainment Conquered Reality*. New York: Knopf, 1998.

Hale, Jonathan. *The Old Way of Seeing*. Boston: Houghton Mifflin, 1994.

Halttunen, Karen. *Confidence Men and Painted Women*. New Haven, CT: Yale University Press, 1982.

Bibliography

Hedges, Chris. *War Is a Force That Gives Us Meaning.* New York: Public Affairs, 2002.

Hiss, Tony. *The Experience of Place.* New York: Knopf, 1990.

Horowitz, Daniel. *The Anxieties of Affluence: Critiques of American Consumer Culture.* Amherst: University of Massachusetts Press, 2004.

Karr, Mary. *The Liar's Club.* New York: Viking Press, 1995.

Kaye, Myrna. *Fake, Fraud, or Genuine?* Boston: Little, Brown, 1991.

Latour, Bruno. *Politics of Nature: How to Bring the Sciences into Democracy.* Cambridge, MA: Harvard University Press, 2004.

Lehman, David. *Signs of the Times: Deconstruction and the Fall of Paul de Man.* New York: Poseidon Press, 1991.

Leopold, Aldo. *A Sand County Almanac.* New York: Ballantine Books, 1970.

MacCannell, Dean. *The Tourist: A New Theory of the Leisure Class.* New York: Schoken Books, 1976.

Mann, Charles C. *1491: New Revelations of the Americas Before Columbus.* New York: Knopf, 2005.

Mansfield, Howard. *The Same Ax, Twice: Restoration and Renewal in a Throwaway Age.* Hanover, NH: University Press of New England, 2000.

Marx, Leo. *The Machine in the Garden: Technology and the Pastoral Ideal in America.* New York: Oxford University Press, 2000.

McKibben, Bill. *The End of Nature.* New York: Random House, 1989.

Melville, Herman. *Moby-Dick.* 1851. New York: Random House, 1992.

Messud, Claire. *The Emperor's Children.* New York: Knopf, 2006.

Mitchell, Don. *Cultural Geography: A Critical Introduction.* Malden, MA: Blackwell Publishing, 2000.

Obama, Barack. *The Audacity of Hope: Thoughts on Reclaiming the American Dream.* New York: Crown, 2006.

Orvell, Miles. *The Real Thing: Imitation and Authenticity in American Culture 1880–1940.* Chapel Hill: University of North Carolina Press, 1989.

Peale, Norman Vincent. *The Power of Positive Thinking.* New York: Prentice-Hall, 1952.

Penn, Mark J., with E. Kinney Zalesne. *Microtrends: The Small Forces Behind Tomorrow's Big Changes.* New York: Twelve, 2007.

Percy, Walker. *The Moviegoer.* New York: Knopf, 1961.

Peterson, Chester, Jr., and Rod Beemer. *Ford N Series Tractors.* Osceola, WI: MBI Publishing, 1997.

Pollan, Michael. *Second Nature.* New York: Atlantic Monthly Press, 1991.

Purdy, Jedediah. *For Common Things: Irony, Trust, and Commitment in America Today.* New York: Knopf, 1999.

Reich, Charles A. *The Greening of America: How the Youth Revolution Is Trying to Make America Livable.* New York: Random House, 1970.

Rich, Frank. *The Greatest Story Ever Sold: The Decline and Fall of Truth from 9/11 to Katrina.* New York: Penguin Press, 2006.

Riesman, David, with Nathan Glazer and Reuel Denney. *The Lonely Crowd: A Study of the Changing American Character.* New York: Doubleday, 1954.

Schickel, Richard. *Intimate Strangers: The Culture of Celebrity in America.* Chicago: Ivan R. Dee, 1985.

Sennett, Richard. *The Fall of Public Man.* New York: Knopf, 1977.

Shepard, Paul. *Man in the Landscape: A Historic View of the Esthetics of Nature.* New York: Knopf, 1967.

Shi, David E. *The Simple Life.* New York: Oxford University Press, 1985.

Thoreau, Henry D. *Walden, or Life in the Woods.* 1854. Boston: Houghton Mifflin, 1929.

Tolle, Eckhart. *A New Earth: Awakening to Your Life's Purpose.* New York: Penguin, 2006.

Trilling, Lionel. *Sincerity and Authenticity.* Cambridge, MA: Harvard University Press, 1973.

Trow, George W. S. *Within the Context of No Context.* New York: Atlantic Monthly Press, 1981.

Urry, John. *Consuming Places.* New York: Routledge, 1997.

Velleman, David J. *Self to Self: Selected Essays.* New York: Cambridge University Press, 2006.

Bibliography

Warhol, Andy. *The Philosophy of Andy Warhol.* New York: Harcourt Brace Jovanovich, 1975.

Weisman, Alan. *The World Without Us.* New York: St. Martin's Press, 2007.

Whisnant, David E. *All That Is Native and Fine.* Chapel Hill: University of North Carolina Press, 1983.

Williams, Bernard Arthur Owen. *Truth and Truthfulness: An Essay in Genealogy.* Princeton, NJ: Princeton University Press, 2004.

Williams, Raymond. *The Country and the City.* New York: Oxford University Press, 1973.